CHURCHLESS

Understanding Today's
Unchurched and How
to Connect with Them
Based on Surveys by Barna Group

Churchless

Barna Group
George Barna &
David Kinnaman
General Editors

TYNDALE®
MOMENTUM
An Imprint of
Tyndale House Publishers, Inc.

BARNA
AN IMPRINT OF TYNDALE MOMENTUM

Visit Tyndale online at www.tyndale.com.

Visit Tyndale Momentum at www.tyndalemomentum.com.

Visit the Churchless website at www.barna.org/churchless.

TYNDALE, Tyndale Momentum, and the Tyndale Momentum logo are registered trademarks of Tyndale House Publishers, Inc. Tyndale Momentum is an imprint of Tyndale House Publishers, Inc. Barna and the Barna logo are trademarks of George Barna. BarnaBooks is an imprint of Tyndale Momentum.

Churchless: Understanding Today's Unchurched and How to Connect with Them

Designed by Alberto C. Navata Jr. and Beth Sparkman

Published in association with the literary agency of Fedd and Company, Inc., doing business at PO Box 341973, Austin, TX, 78734.

Library of Congress Cataloging-in-Publication Data

Churchless : understanding today's unchurched and how to connect with them : based on surveys by Barna Group / Barna Group ; George Barna and David Kinnaman, general editors.

    pages cm
  Includes bibliographical references.
  ISBN 978-1-4143-8709-3 (hc)
1. Non church-affiliated people. 2. Evangelistic work. I. Barna, George, editor.
II. Barna Group.
  BV4921.3.C48 2014
  277.3'083—dc23   2014018281

Printed in the United States of America

20   19   18   17   16   15
7   6   5   4   3

Table of Contents

If we perceive the gap

between "us" and "them"

as W I D E and

essentially uncrossable,

we are less likely

to get close enough

to offer ourselves

in real relationships.

GEORGE BARNA
AND DAVID KINNAMAN,
Churchless

The rise of churchlessness in America

  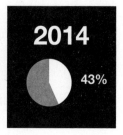

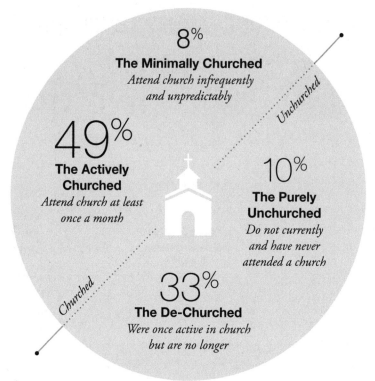

8%
The Minimally Churched
*Attend church infrequently
and unpredictably*

49%
**The Actively
Churched**
*Attend church at least
once a month*

Unchurched

10%
**The Purely
Unchurched**
*Do not currently
and have never
attended a church*

33%
The De-Churched
*Were once active in church
but are no longer*

Churched

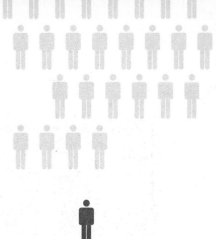

1

IS CHURCHLESSNESS A CRISIS?

Why People Leaving Churches Matters to the Church

If you are like many churchgoers, you have mixed feelings about the unchurched in America.

You may often feel sorry for the churchless, knowing they are missing out on the special experiences and relationships accessible only through the community of people devoted to following Jesus Christ. At other times you may envy them, wishing to flee your church ties and be free, like the unchurched, from the petty jealousies, impractical teaching, second-rate events, and hypocritical behaviors you sometimes witness in congregational life.

You may feel frustrated and helpless in the face of many unchurched folks' self-imposed distance from the love and forgiveness of Christ, and agonize over their inability to live a consistently moral and meaningful life without a deeper understanding of God's ways. Yet occasionally you may wonder if the only distinction between churchgoers and the unchurched is merely a Sunday attendance record.

You might focus on the challenge of reaching the churchless with the gospel and motivating them to attend religious events. Or perhaps, at least some of the time, you get on with your life without giving the spiritual condition of the unchurched much thought, realizing they are human beings with free will who do not want to be anyone's religious project.

Most churchgoers have a sense that involving outsiders in a vibrant community of faith would enhance and improve their lives, while at the same time help Christ's disciples to satisfy some element of the Great Commission. However, that sense—whether it's from duty or love for others— doesn't make the task any easier. Knowing how to connect with those who have chosen to ignore churches, how to successfully invite them to engage with a community of faith, is a challenge that eludes simple, step-by-step solutions.

It is our hope that this book will help you and your faith community feel more empowered to approach and connect with unchurched people. We've done a lot of homework on the churchless population and believe that what we have discovered will help you to be more confident and effective at building bridges between outsiders and your faith community. Our hope is that the information in these pages will give you insights that enable you to create deeper, more enduring relationships with the unchurched people you encounter, leading to their positive introduction to and lasting relationship with Jesus.

Interpreting Culture

We have spent a significant chunk of our lives—nearly sixty years between the two of us—trying to understand culture. The ongoing work of Barna Group affords us the unique opportunity to speak both to our fellow believers about the broader culture and to church outsiders who want to understand the faith community. We take seriously our role as interpreters, and always seek to give as accurate an accounting of reality as possible.

One substantial reality is the growing sense among North American Christians that the culture is changing faster than we can keep up with or respond to—and we're not always sure how to live faithfully in a world that feels like it's headed off the rails. Not too many years ago, church attendance and basic Bible literacy were the cultural norm, and being a Christian didn't feel like swimming against the cultural current. But now?

Churchless confirms that the world has, indeed, altered in significant ways during the last few decades. It's not just your imagination. Real data confirm how drastically the moral, social, and spiritual lives of Americans have changed and are changing. We'll lay these data out for you as accessibly as we can, with plenty of charts and tables so you can see for yourself the trajectory of the changes over time.

But numbers only go so far—knowledge and wisdom are related, yet different, things—and so in these pages you will also find cultural analysis that can help you in your efforts to live a Christ-honoring life in the midst of these massive changes, especially in relation to your non-Christian peers, neighbors, coworkers, and family. One of the things we will suggest again and again is to embrace the churchless—whether they are following Jesus and disconnected from a local church, or not following Jesus at all—as people from whom we can (and must) learn.

Dietrich Bonhoeffer, the German pastor and martyr at the hands of the Nazis, observed that "the church is the church only when it exists for others"—that is, for outsiders. This is an identity that will be difficult to live if we imagine the churchless to be aliens and strangers to our values and priorities. If we perceive the gap between "us" and "them" as wide and essentially uncrossable, we are less likely to get close enough to offer ourselves in real relationships. And that is a significant problem: We hear again and again, both from the unchurched and from local churches that are deeply engaged with the unchurched in their communities, that loving, genuine relationships are the only remaining currency readily exchanged between the churched and the churchless.

For the sake of the life-changing message of Jesus, and of the Great Commission to share that message entrusted to us, the Christian community has an obligation to understand the unchurched. It is our prayer that *Churchless* will give you the knowledge and wisdom you and your faith community need to reach out with renewed joy to the unchurched in your sphere of influence. We believe that now, more than ever, it is urgent for church leaders and all Christians to understand cultural dynamics, to understand the times (see 1 Chronicles 12:32), in order to respond as God's people.

Who Are the Churchless?

Since its inception in 1984, Barna Group has collected data and provided insight about the intersection of faith and culture, including about American adults unconnected to traditional congregations or other faith communities. This book builds on our rich history by updating our tracking research. Through the data, you'll catch a crystal clear glimpse of our culture, today's congregations, and adults who are "outsiders." During the past three decades we have conducted tens of thousands of interviews with unchurched people to discover their hurts, needs, and hopes, with the aim of equipping the church to become more effective at connecting with them. While resources we have previously provided have explained many facets of life among the churchless,[1] the rapidly changing values and lifestyles of the nation's population demand a more current exploration of who unchurched people are today, and how Christians can more accurately understand them and build spiritually meaningful relationships with them.

This book is based on data drawn from a series of eighteen nationwide surveys we conducted with adults between 2008 and 2014.[2] Those studies encompassed interviews with 20,524 American adults, including 6,276 unchurched adults. The insights and analysis we offer in the following pages are not based on the experience of a single church in a particular location, or on a series of anecdotes that support a preexisting hypothesis. The information here is borne from the perceptions, beliefs, behaviors, choices, experiences, expectations, and hopes of a nationally representative body of carefully qualified adults.

US Churched and Unchurched Adults

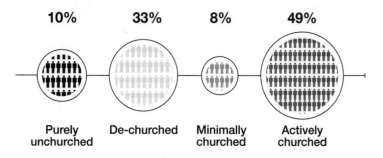

10%	33%	8%	49%
Purely unchurched	De-churched	Minimally churched	Actively churched

So who are the churchless? We define an unchurched person as someone who has not attended a Christian church service, other than a special event such as a wedding or funeral, at any time during the past six months. In the very simplest of terms, think of the *churched* as connected, even if only tangentially, to a church and the *unchurched* as disconnected from a church. The temptation is to think of these as discrete, dichotomous groups—you're either in or you're out. But the truth is that church involvement is more like a continuum, from the most heavily engaged on one end to the most openly hostile on the other, with tens of millions falling somewhere in the middle. Our data show that American adults fall into four broad segments when it comes to their relationship to a church:

- The *actively churched* are those who attend church regularly, usually once a month or more often. Based on our 2014 tracking data, this group represents 49 percent of the adult population.

- The *minimally churched* are those who attend several times a year, but whose appearances in church buildings are infrequent and often unpredictable. The exception to the predictability factor is the group we affectionately label "CEOs," a reference to their tendency to show up at Christmas and Easter Only. The minimally churched constitute about 8 percent of all adults.

- The *de-churched* are those who have been churched in the past but are currently on hiatus. Many of these people have a history of cyclical church attendance patterns, going through a phase when they are involved followed by a phase when they aren't, and so forth. The de-churched are the fastest growing segment, presently one-third of the population.

- The *purely unchurched* are people who have never attended a Christian church service. Because the

United States is one of the most churched nations in
the world, the purely unchurched are relatively rare
in the US religious landscape—just 10 percent of the
adult public. However, within the next decade or so,
as Mosaics and the generation after them become
adults in a culture increasingly hostile to Christian
churches, it is likely this group will become the fastest
growing of the four church-attendance segments.

Our research examines a broad range of life conditions: values, beliefs, lifestyle choices, religious behaviors,
future hopes, experiences, and the like. Based on our data,
Churchless compares the backgrounds, behaviors, and beliefs
of the churched and the unchurched. Throughout the book,
we combine the de-churched and the purely unchurched
segments into the broader category of "unchurched" adults.
When significant differences between these subgroups are
noteworthy, such distinctions will be highlighted.

How Can Data Help?

To grasp the urgency facing churches in America, consider
a few facts about church attendance and the unchurched
population:

- The proportion of unchurched adults has risen (and
  continues to rise) since the Atheist Renaissance in
  America took hold at the dawn of the twenty-first
  century. The energetic anti-God evangelism of Sam

Harris, Richard Dawkins, Christopher Hitchens, and others has emboldened millions of Americans, especially those under forty, to question the existence of God, the role of faith, the value of churches, and the genesis of moral standards. [In the early 1990s, about three out of ten adults were churchless. In the next decade, the figure inched up to one-third of the population. During the current decade, the figure has jumped to 43 percent of all US adults.]

- There is not a single demographic for which church attendance is on the increase. While a few segments have demonstrated relative stability in church attendance levels over the past two decades, most people groups in the United States show declines in attendance. And because young adults have the highest levels of church avoidance, their children are less likely to attend churches, increasing the likelihood that they, too, will avoid churches in adulthood.

- The raw number of unchurched people in the United States is staggering. Most of what gets counted as "church growth" is actually transfer growth rather than conversion growth—that is, people transferring their allegiance from one church to another, not transitioning from non-Christian to Christ-follower. If churches hope to grow their attendance numbers by discipling new believers, they must improve their ability to attract those who are intentionally avoiding a connection with a church.

How can our data help slow or reverse these trends? After all, there is no secret sauce, magic bullet, perfect panacea, or failure-proof formula that will help every church in every environment successfully reach out to the unchurched. In other words, you will not find in these pages the eight steps guaranteed to convert people from antichurch antagonists to pro-church advocates. Outreach that is effective in one setting often flops elsewhere; what works for a fundamentalist Baptist church reaching Boomers and Elders in rural Arkansas will likely fall flat for a postmodern nondenominational congregation reaching out to twentysomethings in San Francisco.

Yet both of those ministries—and yours—can benefit from a better understanding of adults who intentionally avoid Christian churches. God has called you and your faith community to expand his Kingdom in a particular place with unique features and cultural quirks. Translate the research insights you find here into practical, culturally appropriate action. Begin by thinking critically with your church family about how the churchless in your neighborhood, town, or city compare to the representative sample from which this research is drawn. (If you're not sure, brainstorm ways to get to know some unchurched folks!) Start a conversation about how your church engages with the unchurched and de-churched in your community, and about what needs to change to help you be more effective. Then, with a renewed sense of mission and a more focused vision for outreach, get to work.

Barna Group's vision is *to provide people with credible*

knowledge and clear thinking, enabling them to navigate a complex and changing culture. It is our prayer that the information and analysis you find in this book will enable you not only to navigate a complex culture . . . but also to transform it.

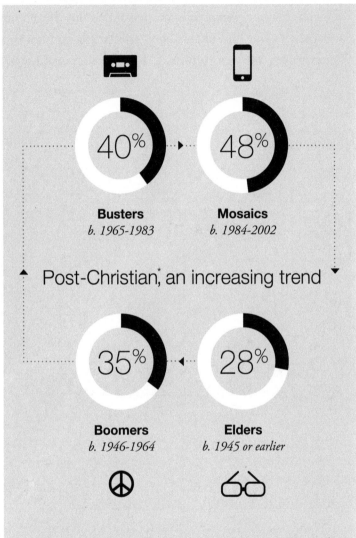

Busters
b. 1965-1983

Mosaics
b. 1984-2002

Post-Christian,* an increasing trend

Boomers
b. 1946-1964

Elders
b. 1945 or earlier

*Based on 15 metrics related to faith, which speak to the lack of Christian identity, belief, and practice.

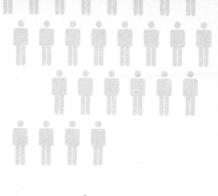

2

OUR CULTURAL MOMENT

What Is Different about Our Time

When we're focused on our own church experience and busy with our own ministries, it's easy to assume unchurched adults are just the same as they ever were. And if that's true, then what has always worked to bring them to church will work as well as it always has.

But with the aid of solid tracking research—a sort of cultural time-lapse photography—we can discern real and significant shifts in people's attitudes, assumptions, allegiances, and behaviors. If we want to understand how to make a difference in our time for the sake of the gospel, we need a firm grip on what is happening. At Barna Group, we sometimes describe ourselves as "reality recognition artists." We believe that reality is our friend. Unfortunately, it is hard for many of us to accept reality, especially when it disagrees with our pre-conceived notions and pet theories. That's why solid research can help. Properly collected and well-analyzed data can take us above our limited, subjective experiences and give us a bird's-eye view of the vast changes that have taken place in our collective culture.

Barna tracking research confirms that substantive changes have, in fact, occurred among the nation's churchless adults over the last several decades. Here's the big picture: Today's unchurched are much less likely to come from a church background than ever before. Furthermore, the unchurched of today have different expectations of church involvement from those of previous decades. In this chapter, we hope to provide an overview of how the churchless today are different from their counterparts in the past when it comes to their attitudes toward the church. But first, let's explore some of the ways our cultural landscape has changed for all of us, churched and churchless alike.

How Our Culture Is Changing

Secularization on the Rise

Imagine a continuum of cultural responsiveness to Christianity (see the following illustration). At the far left end of the continuum is antagonism toward Christianity and churches; at the far right is advocacy. The various points in between—rejection, resistance, and doubt to the left; indifference in the middle; and curiosity, interest, and engagement to the right—convey the positions people in our culture take toward Christianity and communities of Christian faith.

The Christian Faith/Church Adoption Continuum

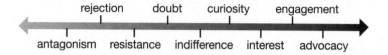

This continuum could serve as the base for a curve on which we might plot the status of America's adults, both churched and churchless. The resulting curve would illustrate the entire population's balance of secular and biblical thinking and behavior. To gain insight into where the curve falls on such a continuum today, we created an aggregate, multidimensional metric designed to assess the level of what we call post-Christian culture in America. The scale is independent of how people categorize themselves. Instead, the measure is based on fifteen different variables related to people's identity, beliefs, and behaviors, including belief in God, church attendance, beliefs about the Bible's accuracy, and likelihood of volunteering at or donating to a church. To be classified as post-Christian, an individual satisfied 60 percent or more of the factors (nine or more out of fifteen). Highly post-Christian individuals—who fall on the antagonism-rejection end of the continuum—met 80 percent or more of the factors (twelve or more out of fifteen).[3]

When we applied this metric to the population at large in January 2013, we learned that nearly two-fifths (38 percent) of the nation's adult population qualifies as post-Christian. That includes 10 percent of Americans who are highly post-Christian—that is, lacking engagement in twelve or more of the measures of belief, practice, or commitment. Another one-quarter (28 percent) was moderately post-Christian, landing on the resistance-doubt-indifference area of the continuum. Examined over time, the research shows that the proportion of highly secularized individuals is growing slowly but steadily.

In other words, in spite of our "Christian" self-descriptions, more than one-third of America's adults are essentially secular in belief and practice. If nothing else, this helps explain why America has experienced a surge in unchurched people—and presages a continuing rise in this population.

Among the churchless, the proportions skew even more heavily to the left of the continuum. Overall, more than three-quarters of unchurched adults fall in the heavy-to-moderate range on the secularization scale. That compares to about one out of eight among the churched. Skeptics lead the secularization march: 74 percent are heavily secularized and 98 percent are in the moderate or higher category. (Barna Group classifies religious commitments into five categories: evangelicals, born-again Christians, notional Christians, adherents of non-Christian faiths, and skeptics. For comprehensive descriptions of these population segments, see chapter 6.)

As you might expect, the data show some striking

generational differences when it comes to secularization, suggesting we should expect a continued shift away from a "Christian nation" in the years to come. The pattern is indisputable: The younger the generation, the more post-Christian it is. Nearly half (48 percent) of Mosaics qualify as post-Christian compared to two-fifths (40 percent) of Busters, one-third (35 percent) of Boomers, and one-quarter (28 percent) of Elders. (Mosaics, sometimes called Millennials, are those born between 1984 and 2002. Busters were born between 1965 and 1983, Boomers between 1946 and 1964, and Elders in 1945 or earlier.) This pattern corresponds to the increasing number of skeptics, particularly in the younger generations.

Estimates of Secularization

People Group	Level of Secularization		
	High	Moderate	Total
All US adults	10%	28%	38%
All unchurched	28	49	77
All churched (attended once or more in the past month)	<1	12	12
Born again	*	8	8
Notional Christians	4	45	49
Other-faith adherents	12	51	63
Skeptics (atheist/ agnostic)	74	24	98

Source: Barna Group
*Indicates less than one-half of one percent

The transition to a post-Christian mind-set and lifestyle has not happened overnight, of course. The secularization of America began decades ago—perhaps triggered by the rebellion of the Baby Boomers in the 1960s—and has continued to gain momentum into the twenty-first century. We can certainly trace the increase of rebellious attitudes and behaviors over the past fifty years—and as today's young adults show, secularization is the norm, not the exception.

Everything Digital

In the last two decades, three network television stations have morphed into hundreds of digital channels. A handful of reading formats—newspapers, books, magazines—have given birth to new media (e-readers, websites) and social media (blogs, Facebook, Twitter). With DVRs, digital season passes, massive multiplayer online gaming, and tablet computers, consumers—both churchless and churched alike—have access to more content and information than anyone could hope to absorb and assimilate. So much demands our attention that, as a culture, we are experiencing an epidemic of distraction. Virtually every facet of our lives receives less concentrated attention than it did two decades ago.

People are more likely than ever to feel they are too busy. They have more commitments, more activities (online and off) that chew up valuable time. When you combine increasing indifference toward church and a culture of short attention spans, you get a lot of people who think they don't have time for church. You also end up with less frequent face time to reach the churchless and form the worldviews of the churched.

Another aspect of the digital shift is the expectation, especially among young people, that they can and should contribute, not just consume. Online technologies such as Instagram, YouTube and Vimeo, BuzzFeed and Reddit, even fan fiction forums, enable any connected person to add his or her image, idea, or opinion to the digital mix. If you consider how most churches deliver content—appointing one person as the authority and encouraging everyone else to sit (consume) quietly while he or she speaks—it is easy to see how that delivery system may come into conflict with changing cultural expectations.

One big upside to digital connectedness is access to people, ideas, and information from all over the world. Twenty years ago, churchgoers had to wait for a visit from the missionaries they supported to learn about the Kingdom impact being made around the world. Today, Christians from opposite sides of the globe can connect with each other on Facebook and Twitter, or through video calling services such as Skype and FaceTime. The church stretches from one corner of the earth to the other, and for the first time, believers can worship together and fellowship with one another in spite of the many miles that separate them.

Many churches are reaching out digitally through websites, podcasts, and social media. The data suggest these tools may be making incremental gains with young churchgoers, but rarely finding traction with churchless adults. This is, in large part, because young unchurched adults don't search for much spiritual content: Just 6 percent report going online to search for faith-related information in a typical week. Faith communities might do well to consider how to channel their digital resources toward engaging with and equipping young Christians to connect with their fellow digital natives.

Changing Self-Perceptions

Barna tracking data since the early 2000s show shifts in how Americans see themselves. While a healthy majority (82 percent) say they are happy, this is a 10 percentage point decrease from a decade ago, when 92 percent of Americans defined themselves in that way. With diminished happiness has come rising loneliness—in the early 2000s, just 12 percent reported being lonely; today, that percentage has grown to 20 percent—as well as stress. A decade ago, 29 percent of adults reported being stressed out. After 9/11, Hurricane Katrina, wars in Afghanistan and Iraq, and the Great Recession of 2008, whose effects are still being felt across the country, 35 percent of Americans now define themselves as stressed out. In addition, the number of people who are concerned about the future has risen substantially, from 64 percent at the turn of the century to 77 percent today.

It is interesting to note that as a culture we have become lonelier even as we have become more connected. In 2012, MIT professor Sherry Turkle gave a TED Talk on the release of her book *Alone Together: Why We Expect More from Technology and Less from Each Other*.[4] Fifteen years before, Turkle had given one of the first TED Talks, hailing the possibility of social media that would bring people together and help them build deep and lasting relationships through online technology. But after a decade and a half studying the effects of social media on individuals and relationships, Turkle's views have radically changed. Instead of noting greater connectedness and deeper relationships, her findings reveal that dissatisfaction and alienation have risen in tandem with our adoption of social media.[5]

The group most likely to see themselves as lonely, stressed out, and concerned about the future is the unmarried, whether divorced or never headed to the altar. While marriage is not the solution to every problem (as any married person can tell you), it is likely we will see these psychographic markers increase if the cultural popularity of marriage continues to decline.

How Attitudes toward Church Are Changing

Churchgoing No Longer Mainstream

Churchgoing is slowly but incontrovertibly losing its role as a normative part of American life. In the 1990s, roughly one out of every seven unchurched adults had never experienced regular church attendance. Today, that percentage has increased to nearly one-quarter. Buried within these numbers are at least two important conclusions: (1) church is becoming increasingly unfamiliar to millions of Americans, and yet (2) the churchless are still largely comprised of *de-churched* adults.

This latter conclusion may be hard for many churchgoing Christians to believe. But it's true: Even though the cultural trend is toward less church-friendliness overall, the vast majority of unchurched adults still have at least some level of personal experience in a church.

Churchgoing Is Losing Traction

Percentage of all US adults

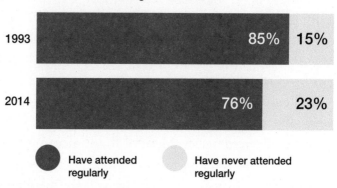

1993 — 85% | 15%

2014 — 76% | 23%

● Have attended regularly   ○ Have never attended regularly

Source: Barna Group annual OmniPoll

Skepticism toward the Contribution of Churches to Society

Most unchurched adults in the United States perceive churches with benign favorability or indifference. When asked if they believe whether a church is a favorable or an unfavorable presence in a community, most churchless adults are either mildly positive or indifferent. One-fourth (28 percent) of the unchurched are very favorable toward churches and two-fifths (38 percent) are somewhat favorable. Another one-fourth (28 percent) express a neutral opinion of churches today. Only 7 percent of unchurched adults believe that a church is a negative factor for a community.

Tracking data show that views about local churches have not changed substantially in the last two decades. Today's churchless adults are not remarkably less favorable toward churches in their community; if anything, there is simply a growing "yawn," with 25 percent expressing they don't know whether they have favorable or unfavorable impressions. This is up slightly from 21 percent in 1993. Yet the research also provides insights into those who are least favorable toward local churches. This includes men, Mosaics (ages eighteen to thirty), never-marrieds, residents of the Northeast, atheists and agnostics, non-registered voters, and Asians. On the other hand, women, Elders (sixty-nine-plus), divorced adults, residents of the South, born-again Christians, and political conservatives are among the most favorable toward churches.

Although many of the churchless hold positive views of churches, a substantial number also have no idea what Christians have accomplished in the nation, either for the better or for the worse. When the unchurched were asked to describe what they believe are the positive and negative contributions of Christianity in America, almost half (49 percent) could not identify a single favorable impact of the Christian community, while nearly two-fifths (37 percent) were unable to identify a negative impact. Of those who could identify one way Christians contribute to the common good, the unchurched appreciate their influence when it comes to serving the poor and disadvantaged (22 percent), bolstering morals and values (10 percent), and helping people believe in God (8 percent). Among those who had a complaint about Christians in society, the unchurched were least favorably disposed toward violence in the name of Christ (18 percent), the church's stand against gay marriage (15 percent), sexual abuse scandals (13 percent), and being involved in politics (10 percent).

Greatest Success/Positive Contribution of Christian Population to America

Question: What has been the greatest success or positive contribution of the Christian population to America during the past few years?

	Churched	Unchurched
Helping people believe in God/evangelism	21%	8%
Having traditional morals/values	17	10
Preventing abortion	6	4
Opposing gay marriage; importance of traditional marriage	7	5
Serving the poor/underprivileged	17	22
None/no positive contributions	8	16
Not sure	18	33
N =	541	368

Source: Barna Group annual OmniPoll 2-10, August 2010, N=1002. Survey also included minimally churched.

Greatest Failure/Negative Contribution of Christian Population to America

Question: What has been the greatest failure or negative contribution of the Christian population to America during the past few years?

	Churched	Unchurched
People committing acts of violence/hate in the name of Christ	21%	18%
Too political, should not be involved in politics	13	10
Against gay marriage, keeping gays from getting married	13	15
Sexual abuse scandal in the Catholic church	12	13
Need to be more outspoken, stand up for important issues, be more assertive	3	1

continued on next page

Don't reflect Christ/don't stand up for Christ/losing standards and becoming more like the world	3	1
Critical/intolerant/bigotry	2	3
None/no negative contributions	12	11
Not sure	14	26
N =	541	368

Source: OmniPoll 2-10, August 2010, N = 1002. Survey also included minimally churched.

While many unchurched cannot name a positive impact of which they are already aware, there are a number of contributions they would like to see from local churches, including helping serve the poor and disadvantaged in the community (25 percent); serving youth, families, and the elderly in their area (14 percent); cultivating biblical values (10 percent); and assisting those in recovery (8 percent).

The Common Good: How Churches Can Contribute Positively to Their Communities

Question: Many churches and faith leaders want to contribute positively to the common good of their communities. What does your community need, if anything, that you feel churches could provide?
(Open-ended query; responses add up to more than 100 percent because respondents could offer more than one answer.)

	Churched	Unchurched
Addressing poverty	31%	25%
Serving youth/families/elderly	11	14
Cultivating biblical values	18	10
Assisting those in recovery	11	8
Doing ministry, introducing people to God	18	6

continued on next page

Addressing workplace, educational, financial issues	9	5
Serving the community	6	3
Being inclusive	3	3
Engaging politically	1	1
Not sure, nothing	9	33
N =	541	368

Source: Barna Group annual OmniPoll 2-10, August 2010, N=1002. Survey also included minimally churched.

Different Expectations of Church Involvement

Another intriguing shift among the churchless has to do with their expectations of church involvement. In the early 1990s, our research showed that nearly seven out of ten adults, if they were to visit a church, would be most interested in attending the Sunday service. Today, weekend worship services remain the most common entry experience, but just slightly; now, only 57 percent of churchless adults say they would be interested in Sunday worship as their starting point. Today's unchurched are more likely to say they are simply not sure, reflecting their disinterest in churches generally, or are more likely to say they would prefer attending some activity other than the Sunday service.

A similar shift is afoot in terms of the number of churches they would attend. The churchless were asked in both 1993 and in 2011 if they would prefer to be involved in one church or multiple churches in their area. Two decades ago, even the unchurched expressed some sense of church loyalty (albeit hypothetical): 85 percent said they would expect to attend just one congregation. The current study reflects a slight loosening of this presumed loyalty, but the more notable shift is among those who don't have a preference or who aren't sure. Together, these percentages doubled from 8 percent to 16 percent, reflecting growing cultural indifference to church involvement.

People Are Less Open to the Idea of Church

Finally, our research shows that the unchurched are becoming less responsive to churches' efforts to connect with them. For example, conventional wisdom says the best way to get people to visit a church is to have friends invite them—and the conventional wisdom is right. The churchless folks we interviewed were most open to "a friend of yours inviting you to attend a local church," with one-fifth expressing strong interest and nearly half willing to consider a church based on this factor. An invitation from a friend is the top-rated way churches can establish connections with the unchurched.

However, while the conventional wisdom remains true today, the road ahead shows challenging signs. Barna Group's trend data raise questions about the long-term durability of this approach. Twenty years ago, two-thirds of churchless Americans were open to being invited to church by a friend. Today, that percentage has slipped to less than half.

It's not only the efficacy of personal invitations that is changing. Barna's tracking data stretching back to the 1990s reveal a slow-growing calcification, or hardening, of the unchurched toward churches. While the churchless continue to show some openness to high-touch, relational connections—pastoral home visits (27 percent), a phone call from a church (24 percent), a survey conducted with them about their interests (21 percent)—they are also increasingly resistant to other forms of outreach. We discovered declines for virtually every type of advertising, including TV, radio, or newspaper (from 20 percent to 18 percent), direct mailings (from 24 percent to 16 percent), and billboard ads (from 21 percent to 14 percent).

Today's Unchurched: More Resistant to Church

Question: There are many different ways a church in your community might let you know more about their church and their services. Let's talk about churches you have never visited before. Would each of the following make you more or less interested in visiting that church? *(Multiple response)*

	1993	2011
A friend of yours invited you to attend a local church	65%	47%
A pastor or a member of a church came to your home to tell you about the church, and invited you to attend	34	27
Someone from a church in your community called you on the phone to tell you about the church, and invited you to attend	34	24
A representative of the church came to your home, conducted a survey about your church attendance and interests, then invited you to attend their church	25	21
You knew a church had a significant online social web presence	N/A	18
You saw or heard advertising for a church on TV, in a newspaper, or on the radio	20	18
You received information about a church through the mail	24	16
You saw advertising for the church on a billboard in your community	21	14

These percentages represent respondents who said the methods would make them either "much more interested" or "a little more interested" in visiting the church.

Reflecting on Change

Our research suggests a growing indifference toward churches among the unchurched. The gap between the churched and the churchless is growing, and it appears that Christian communities of faith will struggle more than ever to engage the outsiders in their neighborhood, town, or city.

Why are some of these changes taking place? Barna research cannot prove causation, given the nature of polling and the complex dynamics of cultural and spiritual change. However, we can point to possible underlying trends. We believe the cultural pressure to tolerate other faith views, to live and let live, is likely one factor. This affects both the churchless (many, as we will see, are reluctant to attach themselves to a group of people perceived as rigid and exclusive) and the churched (who, with good reason, do not want to hurt or offend their unchurched friends).

This dynamic does not mean we should give up inviting our unchurched friends to services and events with our faith community. But it *does* mean we should be wary about "using" our relationships with churchless friends as means to the end of getting them to church. In fact, when we asked pastors and church leaders to share what is working to connect with unchurched people in their surrounding community, Michael Hildago, pastor of a growing church in urban Denver, offered this: "*Listen to them.* I just had someone tell me, 'I never feel like I'm a *project* when I'm at your church.' Rather, people feel embraced and, more importantly, understood, because we do all we can to listen." The key, of course, is loving the churchless for who they are rather than for what they can offer our church, and we'll look at more specific ways to do that in the final chapter. Seeking to genuinely hear and understand someone leaves no room for ulterior motives, and it does sometimes open the door to deeper conversations about faith and Christian community.

John Chandler, who leads a Christian community in Austin, Texas, shared this:

> We've by far had the most success inviting people into our community life by inviting them to serve alongside us. As a matter of fact, that's about the only thing that's worked consistently as far as "official" church activities go. The other thing that has worked is parties—birthday parties, Super Bowl parties—where we invite churched friends and unchurched friends just to connect.

That's quite a bit different from the old standby, "Invite a friend to church on Sunday." Encouraging congregants to invite their friends and family to church remains important, but we also need to examine our underlying motives and our theology of evangelism. Barna data show that American Christians are increasingly resistant to participation in faith-sharing activities. Because of a cultural norm that discourages challenging others' beliefs, many of us are reluctant to witness to those in our sphere of influence. How can we recapture an urgency to fulfill the Great Commission while treating our churchless friends with respect? Wrestling with answers to this question will help prepare your church community to engage more meaningfully with unchurched people.

The cumulative effect of the monumental cultural changes that have swept over us during recent decades is a widening gap, both real and perceived, between the churched and the churchless. To many faithful churchgoers, the unchurched seem increasingly alien and difficult to understand, while the churchless feel ever more comfortable outside a faith community. Yet while the culture will continue to change, our calling as the body of Christ has not and will not. It is our hope that the following chapters will equip you to move forward in ministry and outward in mission.

 Forward Thinking

- What stands out to you the most about the cultural changes that have taken place over the past twenty years? Do you feel primarily wary and skeptical about these changes, or primarily eager and confident? Why?
- What does your church contribute to your community? How do you see the church in the United States impacting the nation?
- What are the main ways your faith community tries to connect with unchurched people? In light of the data regarding how churchless people respond to various methods of connection (such as invitations from friends, phone calls, and advertising), how do you need to change the focus of your efforts to be most effective?

Unchurched Adults Are More Likely to Be...

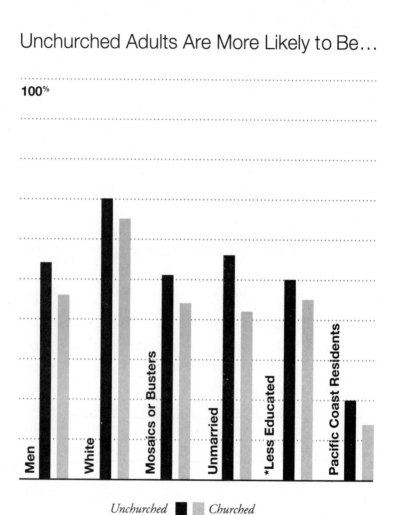

100%

Unchurched ▮ ▮ Churched

Men

White

Mosaics or Busters

Unmarried

*Less Educated

Pacific Coast Residents

*have not gone past high school

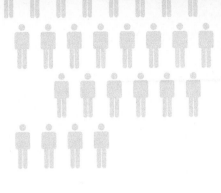

3

PROFILING THE UNCHURCHED

Demographics and Self-Descriptions of Churchless People

Since 2008, we have seen significant reductions in church service attendance, adult Sunday school participation, small group involvement, Bible reading, prayer, personal evangelism, and donations. At the same time, the number of skeptics and adults who are unchurched has increased substantially.

The number of unchurched adults in the United States has increased by more than 30 percent in the past decade. As of 2014, the estimated number of unchurched adults stood at 114 million. Add to that the roughly 42 million children and teenagers who are unchurched and you have 156 million US residents who are not engaged with a Christian church. To put that in context, if all those unchurched people were a separate nation, it would be the eighth most populous country in the world, trailing only China, India, Indonesia, Brazil, Pakistan, Bangladesh, and the remaining churched public of the United States (159 million). It would dwarf every nation in Europe and surpass the population of Japan. Such a precipitous drop in religious behavior should give us pause.

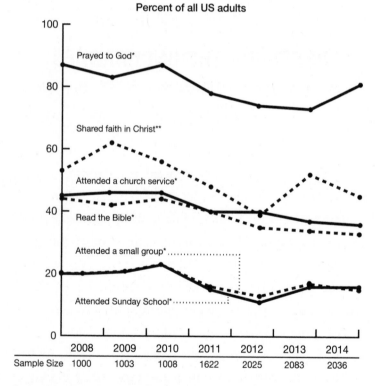

American Religiosity on the Decline
Percent of all US adults

Prayed to God*

Shared faith in Christ**

Attended a church service*

Read the Bible*

Attended a small group*

Attended Sunday School*

	2008	2009	2010	2011	2012	2013	2014
Sample Size	1000	1003	1008	1622	2025	2083	2036

Source: Barna Group annual OmniPoll
* Indicates activity done within the prior seven days
** Indicates activity done by born-again Christians within the past year

Ups and Downs in Faith

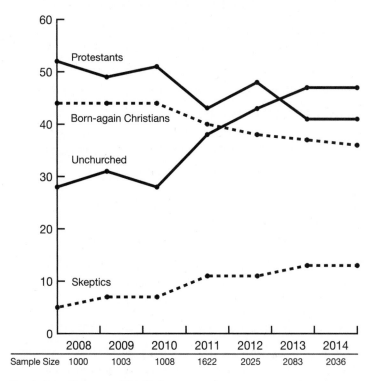

Source: Barna Group annual OmniPoll

In spite of the benefits of being engaged in a community of like-minded spiritual sojourners, millions of American adults make a conscious decision to keep the Christian church at arm's length. In fact, in the past decade, the growth in the number of unchurched adults has been staggering—an increase of about 38 million individuals. That's more people than live in Canada or Australia.

However, the relatively few purely unchurched adults

should serve as a wake-up call. Only about one in ten adults has never attended a Christian church at any time in his or her life, other than for a special service such as a wedding or funeral ceremony. The majority of unchurched individuals have firsthand experience with one or more Christian churches and, based on that sampling, have decided they can better use their time in other ways. This fact should motivate us to examine how our local church looks in the eyes of the de-churched and consider making appropriate changes—not for the sake of enhancing attendance numbers but to address the possibility that we do not always behave like the church Christ died for.

To that end, knowing we must understand the people whom we hope to lead back into the community of Christ-followers, let's dig into the research to better understand who the unchurched are, how they think, how they live, and what they are seeking in life. Just as Jesus meets our needs for forgiveness, acceptance, understanding, belonging, truth, purpose, and much more, perhaps we can better understand and meet the needs of those outside the Christian community, and more effectively engage them in a transformative spiritual experience.

America's churched and unchurched adults have a lot in common: They're people trying to make sense out of life, making the best decisions they can in order to thrive within the framework of their worldview and the opportunities presented to them. Many Christians are surprised to discover that the profile of the unchurched is similar to their own. Granted, some tendencies differ, but these are rarely substantial. In fact, there are no glaring demographic differences between the two groups. In the interest of being comprehensive, however, let's examine some of the marginal demographic distinctions.

A Few Minor Gaps

It remains true that churchless people are somewhat more likely to be men than women (54 percent of the unchurched are men, compared to 46 percent of the churched), but the gap is not huge and has been steadily closing. For instance, in 1994, 58 percent of the unchurched were men. That percentage reached 60 percent in 2003 before it began consistently declining, until stabilizing the last few years around the current level. In other words, the gap between men and women has plummeted from 20 points in 2003 to just 8 points in 2013.

The unchurched tend to have completed fewer years of formal education, but again, the gap is not huge: 50 percent of the unchurched have gone no further than high school graduation, compared to 45 percent of the churched. Overall, 22 percent of the churchless have completed a four-year college degree, only slightly less than the 26 percent among the churched.

Geographically there is a separation of just a few percentage points. The biggest gap is found in the Pacific coast states, where residents comprise 20 percent of the nation's unchurched and 14 percent of the churched. The average gap between the churched and unchurched in all ten US Census divisions is only 2.5 percentage points.

More pronounced are demographic differences related to marriage and age. Although marriage is under siege culturally, it correlates somewhat with church attendance. Among the unchurched, less than half (44 percent) are married, while the number is closer to six out of ten among the churched. A greater proportion of the unchurched (29 percent) than the churched (22 percent) has never been married. Unchurched adults are also about four times more likely to be cohabiting than the churched (11 percent and 3 percent, respectively). Both groups are equally likely to be divorced, separated, or widowed.

The younger a person is, the less likely he or she is to attend church services—though the difference is not as dramatic as you might expect. Overall, 15 percent of unchurched adults are in the 18–30 age bracket (the Mosaic generation), compared to 11 percent of the churched. Thirty-six percent of the unchurched are Busters (born 1965 to 1983), compared to 33 percent of the churched. One-third (33 percent) of the unchurched are Boomers, compared to 35 percent of the churched. One out of every six (16 percent) unchurched adults is an Elder, while just over one-fifth (22 percent) of the churched are among those 69 or older. Most unchurched adults are younger than 50, while most churched adults are over 50. However, the actual age gap is only a few years (a median of 47 years among the unchurched compared to 51 among the churched).

Even the ethnic and racial distinctions that once separated the two groups are no longer as substantial. Overall, 70 percent of the unchurched are white, compared to 65 percent of the churched; 12 percent of the unchurched are Hispanic, compared to 14 percent of the churched; 10 percent of the unchurched are black, compared to 16 percent of the churched; and 6 percent of the unchurched are Asian, compared to 4 percent of the churched.

In 2012, Barna Group partnered with the American Bible Society, the National Hispanic Christian Leadership Conference, and OneHope to produce a comprehensive study of the faith and values of Hispanic and Latino adults, who represent one out of every six US adults—a proportion that will continue to grow in the coming decades. Compared to all Americans, Hispanics report a higher rate of dropping out of church at some point in their lives (67 percent compared to 59 percent among all adults). Unchurched Hispanics are less likely to report very favorable views on Christianity (26 percent compared to 37 percent) and the church (17 percent compared to 31 percent). It is likely that at least some of these less favorable views are related to the child abuse scandals in the Catholic church, given that a majority of Latino adults (68 percent) are Catholic. (If you want to understand more about one of the fastest-growing segments of the US population—and of the churchless population—check out the Barna Group monograph *Hispanic America: Faith, Values & Priorities.*[6])

While a few of the demographic differences between churched and unchurched are statistically significant, we discovered no pattern that delivers mission-critical insight into the thinking and actions of the churchless, or a can't-miss strategy for appealing to them. In fact, the data uncover so many similarities between churched and unchurched people that we have to conclude that a number of stereotypes about both groups are not valid.

In contemporary American society, transcending demographic stereotypes is increasingly feasible. Statistically speaking, for example, it is more likely than ever that a black adult will have an average or above-average household income, or that a woman will be as highly educated as a man. Our common demographic stereotypes need a radical makeover. Status and achievement levels are constantly changing. As discrimination based on gender, age, race or ethnicity, and income has decreased, so have the obstacles that once hindered demographic movement.

Nobody Knows Me Like I Do

A good place to turn for a better understanding of churchless people is to churchless people. Of course, asking others to describe themselves does not generate a completely accurate portrait—we human beings often have a distorted view of ourselves, or intentionally shape our public image to our advantage—but it does provide a reasonable facsimile of who they are.

As is the case with demographics, we discovered by interviewing unchurched folks that many of the stereotypes we hold about them are not valid. Perhaps most significant is that more than one-quarter of the unchurched are seriously interested in matters of faith, and nearly two-thirds have generally positive perspectives on faith matters. Consider the self-identification of unchurched adults:

- 21 percent are born-again Christians

- 21 percent are Pentecostal or charismatic Christians

- 23 percent say they are "absolutely committed" to Christianity

- 26 percent say they are currently on a quest for spiritual truth

- 34 percent describe themselves as "deeply spiritual"

- 41 percent "strongly agree" that their religious faith is very important in their life today

- 51 percent say they are actively seeking something better spiritually than they have experienced to date

- 62 percent consider themselves to be Christian

- 65 percent define themselves as "spiritual" people

These numbers do not paint a portrait of Christian zealots, but neither do they reflect the common stereotype of "Christophobics," people who disdain Christianity and do all they can to belittle it or tear it down. Depending on how we slice the data, there are more than 40 million unchurched adults in the United States who are significantly interested in Christianity—not just as a religious system, but as a values code, a moral standard, a relational base, and a way of life.

The type of spiritual experience and community church-less people are seeking has a decidedly postmodern slant. For example, these are not individuals prone to seeking the "one right way" or absolute moral truth; four out of five admit they are very open to considering moral views different from their own. In addition, social and environmental issues are their priority. More than four out of five say they care deeply about social justice, with half going so far as to say they have a "passion" for social justice. And more than four out of five say they are very concerned about the environment.

Part of the reason the unchurched do not feel as if they are missing out on church life is that they are largely upbeat about the future and believe they can figure things out and make life work. Nearly three out of four are optimistic about their future despite the fact that two-thirds are uncomfortable with the shape the world is in. The churchless are no more likely than churched folks to find themselves in serious financial debt; only one out of six is in financial trouble. Most of them (80 percent) feel "very much at peace with life." A similar proportion believe they live a "simple life," while at the same time, two-thirds say they are totally committed to getting ahead in life. Four out of five want their life to make a difference in the world, and more than three-quarters contend they are clear about their life's meaning and purpose. They are interested in making a local impact, with four out of five saying they want to contribute to the good of their community.

Clearly, the lives of the unchurched are not dissipating into chaos and disappointment. However, not everything is pristine in their world, either. A slight majority admit they would make significant changes in their past or future, given the chance. Less than half feel they have deep "soul connections" with friends. Nearly two out of five claim to be stressed out. And despite claiming clarity about why they live on earth, nearly half (47 percent) admit they are seeking further insights into the meaning and purpose of their life.

Reflections on the Unchurched Profile

As we've seen, unchurched adults are very much like churched adults . . . except they don't attend church. Here are some additional insights based on our research to get you thinking about who they are and how you might better connect with them.

They tend to be culturally savvy, capable of gathering, interpreting, and responding to information in ways that advance their causes, support their dreams, and make sense to them. Brian Wurzell, worship pastor at Hillside Community Church in Rancho Cucamonga, California, believes that "we've got to get better at engaging/investing in technology. The speed of technological advancement has required the church to either stay with it or lose its ground. Churches that are choosing to embrace technology as a medium for the message tend to be the churches thriving."

As part of this book project, we interviewed several dozen pastors from different denominational traditions, church sizes, and cultural contexts to get their on-the-ground perspectives about relating to the unchurched. Pieter

Breytenbach, a pastor in Pretoria, South Africa, highlighted skepticism and technological savvy as hallmarks of church-less adults. We asked, "Do you think the unchurched audience is different today from fifteen years ago? How?" Pieter's answer: "People are a lot more literate and have much more opportunity to research other opinions." This observation aligns with our research. Churchless adults tend to be independent and self-reliant, more skeptical than the churched about the motivations of people and institutions, and ready to stonewall those entities until they prove trustworthy and beneficial. Many do not trust others easily and are not prone to taking statements at face value. When talking with the unchurched, be prepared to back up your claims with persuasive information.

Like their churched counterparts, most unchurched people want to make a difference in the world, leaving their mark on the people or causes that capture their heart and imagination. Many look for other people and groups that care about the same things, and are more likely than churched people to invest themselves in some type of difference-making project. Several of the church leaders we interviewed whose communities are successfully engaging with unchurched people emphasized serving together as one indispensable means of connection (besides being an indispensable activity of living as God's people!). Jason Garcia, pastor of Saddleback San Clemente, told us his congregation invests in "cause-related events that connect with community concerns." Brian Wurzell reiterated that "social responsibility in our city" is a non-negotiable. Often, much of the volunteerism encouraged by churches focuses on serving the church itself. If serving is to be a point of engagement with the churchless, it must be directed outward, to benefit and bless the surrounding community.

 Forward Thinking

- Consider the characteristics of the unchurched as analyzed in this chapter. How does your direct experience with churchless people square with our findings?
- What information about the unchurched surprised you most? Why?
- How have your assumptions or stereotypes regarding unchurched people changed after reading this chapter?

2 in 3 unchurched Americans say they are spiritual people

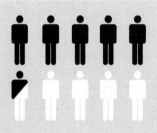

More than half say their faith is very important to their life

99% are aware of Christianity and **69%** hold a favorable view of it

Yet … **nearly half** see no value in personally attending church

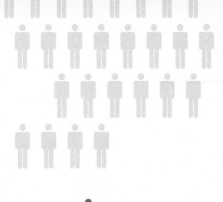

4

PERCEPTIONS OF FAITH, CHRISTIANITY, AND CHURCHES

What Unchurched People Think and Feel about Religion

As a culture on the run, heavily invested in technology and saturated with media messages, we form lasting perceptions based on ten-second video clips, 140-character tweets, fifteen-second sound bites, Instagram snapshots with short captions, and thirty-second commercials. We are too distracted to finish reading the books we start. We select our political leaders based on appearance and demeanor, and on their clever, if vacuous, replies to substantive questions. When asked to discuss the most significant issues of the day, most of us demonstrate only superficial knowledge of—or interest in—world-shaping matters. Yet, armed with minimal depth and concern, we form thousands of enduring impressions that serve as the basis for daily decision making in most areas of our lives.

It's not surprising, then, that churchless people have formed such lasting perceptions of faith in general, of Christianity, of churches, and of Christians. Unfortunately, some of these images stand in the way of a churchgoing Christian's ability to connect with the unchurched in a meaningful and potentially life-changing way.

Images of Faith

Unchurched people have little quarrel with the notion of faith. Two-thirds say they are spiritual people and more than half (57 percent) say their religious faith is very important in their life today.[7] About half also claim to be actively seeking something better spiritually than they have experienced to date. Forty percent of young unchurched adults talk about faith matters with friends and family during a typical week.

Few churchless people are anti-faith or harbor animosity toward God; the unchurched are more disinterested in or unimpressed with faith than hostile to it. (Yet with each new church scandal splashed across the headlines, they are less inclined to see value in a Christian faith community.) A large majority of the unchurched has positive perceptions of Jesus, but most have not deeply considered what impact his life, ministry, death, and resurrection should make on their way of life.

Images of Christianity

While virtually every unchurched person (99 percent) is aware of Christianity—remember, nearly two-thirds still consider themselves to be Christians, and three-quarters were formerly churched—just three out of ten hold a very favorable view of the Christian faith, and an equal proportion hold an unfavorable view. Just 30 percent of the churchless believe it is desirable to be known as a Christian in American society today. While only a slightly higher percentage of churched people hold that view (38 percent), churchgoers are more willing to buck public sentiment and embrace their Christian identity. The unchurched tend to view things differently. Without a definitive sense that participating in a Christian church is valuable, the unchurched may find their willingness to connect more deeply with the faith is inhibited by the negative image of Christians in contemporary culture.

Adding fuel to the fire, a majority of the unchurched agree that "Christianity is no longer the faith that Americans automatically accept as their personal faith." The impression that Christianity is on the decline is increasingly held by both churched and unchurched folks. In a society where reputation and image count for so much, convincing outsiders to align with a group of people who are losing popularity and public trust is a genuine challenge.

Images of Churches

As we have seen, most churchless adults used to be churched. They parted company with their churches for various reasons, but for more than four out of five church avoiders, the decision was conscious and intentional. Motivating them to return is no small task.

Unchurched Adults' Impressions of Denominations and Christianity

Denominational group	Aware	Favorable impression Very	Somewhat	Unfavorable impression	Aware but no opinion	Not aware
Catholic	94%	18%	27%	33%	15%	6%
Baptist	93	21	33	14	23	7
Methodist	90	16	39	9	26	10
Mormon	88	8	22	31	27	12
Presbyterian	84	10	33	9	32	16
Lutheran	79	13	28	11	27	21
Christianity	99	29	40	27	3	1

Source: Barna Group, OmniPolls 1-11 and 1-12, conducted January 2011 and January 2012; sample included 1,535 unchurched adults and 2,112 churched adults

The names and denominational identities of various churches do not spring easily to mind among unchurched people. When asked to identify all of the denominations or religious groups they could recall, they were actually more likely to list non-Christian groups—Judaism (23 percent), Islam (21 percent), Buddhism (10 percent), Mormonism (10 percent), and Hinduism (5 percent)—than leading Christian groups. Among the Christian bodies named, Catholicism led the pack (46 percent), trailed by the generic label "Christianity" (40 percent). Specific denominations remembered were Baptist (18 percent), Lutheran (6 percent), Methodist (6 percent), Presbyterian (4 percent), and Pentecostal or Foursquare (3 percent). As shown in the table,

unchurched folks' perceptions of these Christian groups var-
ied, with the Catholic church (33 percent) and The Church
of Jesus Christ of Latter-day Saints, or Mormons (31 percent)
leading in the unfavorable category, and Methodists (55 percent), Baptists (54 percent), Presbyterians (43 percent), and
Lutherans (41 percent) leading the favorables.

Our surveys reveal that about one-quarter (24 percent)
of the unchurched believe the typical church experience is
boring or tiresome. In addition, they don't see church as
a place of meaningful community. Churchless people are
about 40 percent more likely to say that church services felt
like "a group sharing the same space at a public event, but
not a group of people that was connected to each other in
any real way" than to say services felt like "a group that was
united in belief, cared for and would take care of each other
in practical ways." The subgroups most likely to report this
kind of disconnect within the faith community are adults
under thirty, political liberals, and Hispanics.

The churchless are not completely down on churches,
but they sure aren't cutting them much slack. Consider these
survey results:

- Asked to identify what churches could do to
  contribute to the community's common good,
  few mention the activities most churches major
  on: teaching, worship, and evangelizing. Almost
  all the activities they describe focus on service:
  feeding the needy (30 percent), providing housing
  for the homeless (18 percent), keeping kids off

the streets (11 percent), providing counseling and support groups (11 percent), and clothing the poor (11 percent). More unchurched people recommend accepting non-Christian beliefs as legitimate (11 percent) and accepting others instead of judging them (7 percent) than recommend the activities most churches regularly engage in.

- Six out of ten say they are more likely to develop religious beliefs on their own than to adopt a slate of beliefs or a worldview taught by a church.

- Relatively few of the unchurched express interest in returning to a church or even investigating available churches. One-third say they are "completely open to carrying out and pursuing their faith in an environment or structure that differs from the typical church."

All this data leads us to a direct examination of the reasons the unchurched avoid Christian churches. The biggest issue is a perceived lack of value. In a consumer-oriented society, value is a big issue—a variation on "what have you done for me lately?" Nearly half of churchless people attribute their lack of church attendance to an absence of value. (This figure is the sum of those who say they have no interest, have no reason, are too busy, can practice faith at home, and have not found a church they like. These are different ways of expressing that church involvement has thus far proved of little value to their lives.)

Reasons the Unchurched Avoid Church

Not interested; it's too boring	15%
No particular reason; just lazy; not sure	13
Too busy; have other obligations	11
I am not Christian	10
I don't believe in God/Jesus	10
Christians are hypocrites; they're not genuine	9
I can worship/pray/practice faith from home	6
I'm disillusioned with organized religion	5
I have different (Christian) beliefs than they do	4
All churches want is my money	4
I haven't found one I like/am comfortable with	3
They're too controlling/judgmental	3
I am limited by health issues	3

Source: Barna Group, OmniPoll 1-13, conducted January 2013; sample included 898 unchurched adults

When we asked unchurched people to recall the most recent church service they attended, less than one in ten could identify anything from the experience that they considered insightful, valuable, helpful, or memorable. (Among churched people, about one-third identified something useful from their most recent experience.) In light of these disappointments, it's understandable that returning for more church experiences may not seem particularly worthwhile to the unchurched.

Reflections on the Unchurched's Images of Christianity and Churches

Few of us have a tight grip on "real" reality. That is, our sense of reality is largely shaped—mediated—by the media. A combination of personal experiences and media depictions forms the average American's worldview and perception of reality. Unfortunately, the media depiction of churches is often negative, with fringe groups or ethical scandals getting the most press. A major challenge to local churches is the conflict between their desire to counteract the media's negative portrayals and their desire to act with humility rather than chase accolades for their ministry's good works. This conflict has created an environment where the good work and loving efforts of church people often go unnoticed, while any and everything negative becomes the "news" on which people base their lasting images of churches and Christianity. When unchurched people have had negative or valueless personal experiences of church, counteracting these impressions becomes doubly hard.

One way to change people's minds about your church is to do things in and for your community that are valuable, visible, and memorable. Churched people have more favorable views of the church's value because they have personally experienced the spiritual satisfaction and relational fulfillment that come with involvement in a healthy faith community. In chapter 14 we'll look in more detail at the different ways churches provide value for the people involved in them. But why wait for unchurched people to join your church to offer them a valuable experience? The media's relentless onslaught against faith communities is only believable when it agrees with a person's firsthand experience. What does your church offer to churched and churchless people that is too valuable, too meaningful, for them to ignore?

 ## Forward Thinking

- What surprised you most about unchurched people's perceptions of Christianity and Christian churches? Why?
- What do you think about the gap between most churches' priorities (teaching, worship, evangelism) and what unchurched people believe churches should prioritize (meeting practical needs within the community)? Do you think it's important to close this gap? Why or why not?
- What is one ongoing service or ministry your church could offer to your community that is valuable, visible, and memorable? What obstacles must be overcome to launch and sustain such a ministry? How will you address these challenges?

1/3 of the churchless say they have an active relationship with God that influences their life

They describe that relationship as:

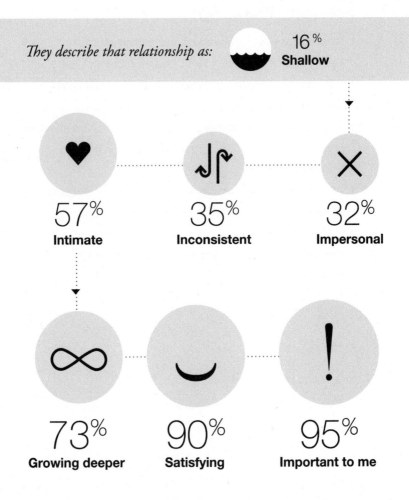

16% **Shallow**

57% **Intimate**

35% **Inconsistent**

32% **Impersonal**

73% **Growing deeper**

90% **Satisfying**

95% **Important to me**

Get full color infographics from this book at www.barna.org/churchless

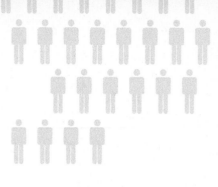

5

DOING FAITH

The Religious Behaviors of Churchless People

By definition, the unchurched do not attend church services—but that does not mean they have abandoned all faith activities. Much of their religious activity is privately undertaken, or pursued within their family or circle of friends.

The Bible

Although many churchless people have little faith in the Bible, as we will see in the next chapter, one of the most common faith-related activities they engage in is reading God's Word. Most unchurched adults own a Bible, and millions of them read it regularly. They may not defend the inerrancy of the Scriptures, but nearly half of them believe that at least some portion of the Bible's content is defensible and valuable.

But owning a book, occasionally reading it, and grasping the content are all different matters. We have two clues that the unchurched are not well educated in biblical content. The first is the many unbiblical beliefs they harbor, which we will look at in more detail in chapter 6. For instance, large numbers of them believe Jesus was a sinner. Most do not believe Satan exists or that an evil spirit influences people's lives. Most are skeptical about the nature of God and do not buy the notion that he is a supernatural, perfect, and dominant being. They have read the stories and know much of the content, but many do not embrace those teachings as fact.

The second clue, revealed by data Barna Group has tracked since 2011, in partnership with the American Bible Society, is that only one out of ten claims to have read the entire Bible. While that is not unusual—most churched people have yet to do so, as well—the unchurched are one-third as likely as the churched to have read all sixty-six books of the Scriptures. It is likely this contributes to some of their theological confusion.

When we asked people to identify the source of information that is most helpful when they are striving to respond to challenging questions about matters of faith, only one-quarter of the churchless mentioned the Bible as their best source. That is half as often as the Bible was mentioned by churched adults.

We might conclude that, while unchurched Americans are likely to own a Bible and to have spent some time reading it, they are generally not attracted to or compelled by what they have been exposed to in God's Word. For some this is due to a lack of tools for interpreting the content. Maybe they are confused about different interpretations they have heard in various churches. Perhaps they own a translation that is hard to understand. Some of them simply ignore the Bible because they have not been exposed to practical applications. There are many reasons churchless people do not appreciate the Bible. The bottom line is, the Bible is generally accepted as legitimate religious literature but not as a useful life resource.

Relating to God

A majority of unchurched adults (58 percent) pray to God during a typical week. For most of them it is a one-way conversation: six out of ten say they do not believe God speaks to them. About one-sixth are certain God speaks to them, with the remaining one-quarter not sure but open to the possibility.

Those who believe God speaks directly to them ascribe various methods of communication to him. Most common are the beliefs that he influences their mind or emotions (35 percent) and that he provides signs (30 percent). Somewhat less common are miraculous or inexplicable circumstances (25 percent); specific guidance given to them by other people, as conduits of God's direction (25 percent); a pointed and personally meaningful Bible passage (24 percent); and personally relevant teaching or preaching (20 percent). Less frequent are personally significant passages read from a book other than the Bible (17 percent) and audible voices or whispers (16 percent).

The perceived silence of God may be related to the fact that only one-third of the churchless have what they consider to be an active relationship with God that influences their life today. The words they use to describe that relationship, though, are telling:

- Important to you . . . . . . 95 percent

- Satisfying . . . . 90 percent

- Growing deeper . . . . 73 percent

- Intimate . . . . 57 percent

- Inconsistent . . . . 35 percent

- Impersonal . . . . 32 percent

- Shallow . . . . 16 percent

One has to wonder why, if their relationships with God are already so fulfilling, this subset of the unchurched would consider participating in a local church—unless a community of faith could show how church engagement can increase the intimacy, constancy, and depth of a relationship with God. (By the way, the biggest difference between the descriptions offered by churched and unchurched people of their connection to God is that church regulars are seventeen percentage points more likely to claim intimacy with God.)

Unchurched adults tend not to invest much energy in deepening their relationship with God. By far the most common effort is to have a time of extended quietness and solitude with God, something that one-third of the churchless say they do. One out of every four says he or she engages in daily worship. One out of five has planned a period of focused, prolonged spiritual reflection. One out of six has undertaken planned times of focused, prolonged prayer. One out of eight occasionally confesses sins, verbally, to another person. Less than one in ten engages in intense Bible study or a significant food fast.

Religious Expression

Private prayer and worship are not the only ways unchurched adults express themselves spiritually. Two-thirds of the churchless admit that during the past month they have tried a variety of things to expand their faith understanding and maturity. Some of those efforts are comparatively common; beyond praying and reading the Bible, discussing faith matters with family and friends and watching religious TV programs led the list. Less common attempts to grow spiritually were listening to Christian music, meditating, seeking counseling, reading spiritual books, and spending time appreciating nature. One-third of the unchurched did nothing to advance their spirituality.

One of the more discouraging survey results is that six out of ten unchurched adults admit the faith they possess today is no different from their spiritual maturity when they were a child. On average, that means they have not grown much, if at all, in more than three decades—a period that may have included years of church involvement.

Reflections on Religious Behaviors

Attending church services is just one of many spiritual endeavors people undertake. To assume that churchless people are irreligious or have no spiritual dynamic is to misunderstand many of them. And this false assumption impacts our potential to connect with the unchurched. Assuming they are spiritually bankrupt will only make us offensive to them.

Another factor to consider is that one-third of all churchless adults are former Catholics who say they will not consider returning to the Catholic church. They retain beliefs in God, Jesus, the Bible, and other elements of Christianity, but are hesitant to shift their allegiance to a Protestant church, which is unfamiliar or even scary to many of them. Walking with these believers into a connection with a local church or a reconnection with a Catholic parish demands sensitivity, trust, patience, and understanding—and the offer of an irresistible reason to pursue that connection.

Certainly another barrier we face is the spiritual lethargy of many unchurched people. They have been absent from the church for years; most have failed to mature. And breaking free from inertia is difficult. They must find a compelling reason to do so, an inspiring vision of what they are missing. Is your faith community casting—and living—such a vision among the unchurched in your neighborhood or city?

Forward Thinking

- What surprises you most about the many religious behaviors practiced by unchurched people? Why?
- How does your church help people increase the intimacy, constancy, and depth of their relationship with God? How could you communicate these benefits to unchurched people?
- How is your church casting—and living—a vision of Christian community that inspires people to connect? What could you do better?

Churchless beliefs on...

Heaven
Believe they'll go to heaven because they've confessed their sins to Jesus and accepted him as their Savior

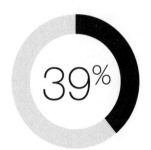

Purpose
Say the purpose of life is to love God with all your heart, soul, mind, and strength

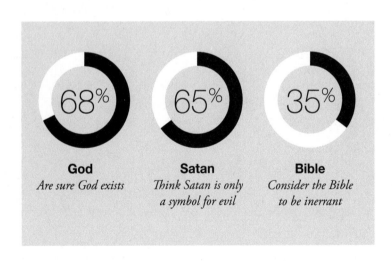

God
Are sure God exists

Satan
Think Satan is only a symbol for evil

Bible
Consider the Bible to be inerrant

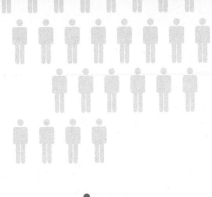

6

THE CREED OF THE CREEDLESS

The Religious Beliefs that Define Unchurched People's Faith

As we've seen, a huge majority of America's unchurched adults have considerable experience with Christianity and Christian churches. Only about one in ten of the unchurched was raised without a significant period of church attendance, and most had a period of church engagement during their adult years as well. Most of their experiences have been in what many consider to be "mainstream Christian churches"—not necessarily the historic mainline denominations, but the "major brands" of modern Christianity. Two-thirds come from Assemblies of God, Baptist, Catholic, Methodist, Lutheran, or Presbyterian backgrounds.

Given that experience, what did they learn and adopt from their exposure to church-based Christianity? Many of their foundational religious beliefs were birthed, developed, or reinforced by the churches they have been involved with over their lifetime. What mix of beliefs have they taken away from those experiences?

Beliefs about God

God has a mediocre reputation with millions of Americans. When asked to choose from a series of possible descriptions of God, four out of five churched people select the "all-knowing, all-powerful, perfect creator of the universe who still rules the world today." However, less than half of the unchurched choose that description. Other views of God's nature—none of which is more popular on its own than the orthodox description—are together more widely accepted by the unchurched than the biblical view. One-fifth of unchurched people contend that "god" refers to "a state of higher consciousness that a person may reach"; one in seven says there is no God; one in ten claims that God "refers to the total realization of personal, human potential"; 4 percent argue that "there are many gods, each with different power and authority"; another 7 percent claim that "everyone is god"; and the remaining 3 percent say they do not know if God exists or how to characterize who or what God is.

The churchless segments least likely to hold a biblical

How the Unchurched Perceive the Nature of God

Percentage of unchurched US adults

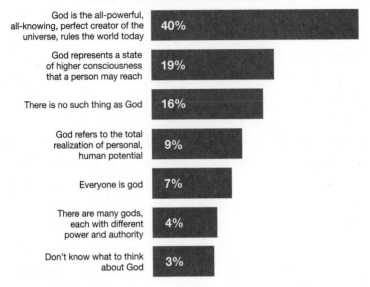

God is the all-powerful, all-knowing, perfect creator of the universe, rules the world today	40%
God represents a state of higher consciousness that a person may reach	19%
There is no such thing as God	16%
God refers to the total realization of personal, human potential	9%
Everyone is god	7%
There are many gods, each with different power and authority	4%
Don't know what to think about God	3%

Source: Barna Group, OmniPoll 1-14, conducted January-February 2014;
N = 945 unchurched adults

understanding of God's nature are the youngest, the most educated, the most liberal, and Asian.

Certainty about the existence of God is not very widespread, either. Fewer than four out of ten unchurched adults are 100-percent certain God exists. On a scale of one to one hundred, representing their level of certainty about the existence of God as described in the Scriptures, the average "certainty score" was 68. Half placed themselves at 90 or higher on the scale. For the sake of context, three-quarters of the churched said they are 100-percent certain about the existence of the God of Israel. On average, churched people scored themselves at 92 on the scale and 84 percent placed themselves at 90 percent or higher.[8]

Jesus Christ is another source of confusion among the churchless. Just half of them have a strong opinion about him one way or the other. Three out of ten strongly agree that "when he lived on earth, Jesus Christ was human and committed sins, like other people do." A slightly smaller number (23 percent) strongly disagree with that characterization of Christ. The rest, roughly half of the group, are undecided about what to make of the alleged holiness of the Son of God. The unchurched adults most likely to contend that he lived a sinless life are blacks, born agains, and those residing in the red states. However, only a minority in each of those groups strongly denied that Jesus Christ was a sinner.

Given their views of God and Jesus, it's not surprising that the third person of the Trinity fares poorly as well. While

Unchurched Views of the Trinity

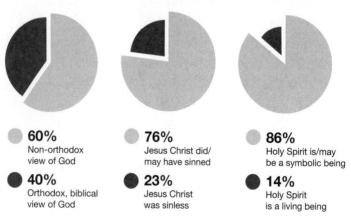

60%
Non-orthodox
view of God

40%
Orthodox, biblical
view of God

76%
Jesus Christ did/
may have sinned

23%
Jesus Christ
was sinless

86%
Holy Spirit is/may
be a symbolic being

14%
Holy Spirit
is a living being

about half of the unchurched either had no opinion or a weak opinion about the nature of the Holy Spirit, the prevailing view was that "the Holy Spirit is just a symbol of God's power or presence, but is not a living entity." More than one-third of the unchurched strongly embraced that description, while just 14 percent strongly rejected it.

Beliefs about Evil

A central theme of Christian theology depicts the war between good and evil as led by God against Satan. It's nigh impossible to fight and win a battle when you don't know your enemy, or don't even believe there is an enemy—yet that is precisely the challenge facing American Christianity today. Not many unchurched adults accept the idea of a living spiritual being known as Satan. Our research consistently shows that two-thirds (65 percent) of unchurched people believe Satan is not a living being but only a symbol of evil.

In fact, the whole concept of negative spiritual influence does not resonate too deeply with the churchless. For instance, less than one out of four strongly believes that a human being can be under the influence of spiritual forces, such as demons or evil spirits. This idea of intermediary influence does not fit well within the worldview of a self-sufficient person, and it undermines the sense of power and control that most Americans strive to maintain.

Black-and-white depictions of a holy God at war with a banished, evil Satan for the souls of people fall mostly on deaf ears among the unchurched. Only one-third believe that people must choose one side or the other—God or Satan—because there is no in-between position. Americans are generally comfortable with shades of gray in most dimensions of life, and the spiritual dimension is no exception.

Closely related to the idea of a battle between good and evil is the concept of how God interacts with our suffering. Consistent with their general dismissal of most things super-natural, the unchurched do not buy into the notion that God is aware of, feels, and shares their pain. Only one-third believe that God has such empathy. One-fifth believe that God may be aware of their pain but do not accept the idea that he feels or shares it with them. Another one-fifth say God is totally oblivious to any pain we feel. About 15 percent dismiss the whole discussion by saying they don't believe God exists, and 11 percent say they have no idea.

Beliefs about the Afterlife

One of the dominant emphases of Protestant churches is addressing what happens after a person dies. Evangelical churches, in particular, stress the importance of accepting Jesus Christ as personal Savior, which provides assurance about one's eternal destination. Most Americans, how-ever, and especially most unchurched adults, do not share the evangelical preoccupation with eternal salvation. Given their theological views on God and Jesus Christ, and their dismissal of the notion that a supernatural war is taking place for the allegiance of their souls, it is not surprising that unchurched adults are indifferent to the importance and means of salvation.

As the table on the following page shows, a bit more than one-third of the unchurched say they have made a personal commitment to Jesus Christ that is still important in their life today. (That is half as many as churched adults.) The commitment is likeliest among those who are more than fifty years of age, who lack a college diploma, are married, are black, describe themselves as socio-political conservatives, and reside in the red states. Noteworthy for their lack of such a commitment are unchurched adults who are Asian (17 percent).

Fifteen percent of the churchless believe that after they die they will go to heaven because they have confessed their sins to Jesus and accepted him as their Savior. We label this group "born-again Christians." A majority of those who have made a personal commitment to Christ, however, have other views about their ultimate destiny. Seven percent of the unchurched who are committed to Christ admit they do not have any idea where they will wind up after their time on earth is done. Five percent believe that, regardless of their commitment to Christ, they will go to heaven because they are "a good person." Smaller groups contend that they will go to heaven after death because "God loves all people and will not let them perish" (3 percent) or that they have earned their salvation by doing their best to obey the Ten Commandments (1 percent).

The Unchurched and Salvation: What They Believe Will Happen After They Die

Have not made a personal commitment to Jesus Christ	61%
Have made a commitment to Christ AND believe they'll go to heaven because they confessed their sins and accepted Jesus as their Savior	15
Have made a commitment to Christ AND believe they'll go to heaven because they are basically a good person	5
Have made a commitment to Christ AND believe they'll go to heaven because they tried their best to obey the Ten Commandments	1
Have made a commitment to Christ AND believe they'll go to heaven because God loves all people and will not let them perish	3
Have made a commitment to Christ AND do not know what will happen to them after they die	7
Have made a commitment to Christ AND possess some other belief	2

Source: Barna Group, OmniPoll 1-14, January-February 2014; N = 945 unchurched adults

In fact, only one out of five churchless adults strongly agrees that a person cannot earn his or her way into heaven. Most contend that heaven is available to anyone who "is generally good, or does enough good things for other people." This is a classic works mentality of salvation and fits comfortably with the American can-do, self-sufficient spirit; it also perhaps reflects a desire for inclusiveness. Women are more likely than men to embrace this thinking, along with those who were raised in Catholic and mainline Protestant churches.

Only 15 percent of the unchurched agree they have a personal responsibility to introduce other people to their religious beliefs—a process churches call evangelism. Twice as many agree that it is important to have "active, healthy relationships with people who belong to religious faiths that do not accept the central beliefs of your faith." Given that their faith is so flexible and open to change, their objective for these associations may be less evangelistic and more relational than is the case among most evangelicals.

Personal Spiritual Commitments

Based on their religious beliefs, people can be grouped together in various ways. Barna Group has pioneered a number of classification approaches to determine where people stand on a particular religious continuum.

One such strategy is to divide people into one of five groups: evangelicals, non-evangelical born-again Christians,

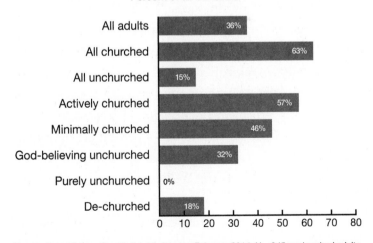

Who Meets the "Born Again" Criteria?
Percent of all US adults

All adults	36%
All churched	63%
All unchurched	15%
Actively churched	57%
Minimally churched	46%
God-believing unchurched	32%
Purely unchurched	0%
De-churched	18%

Source: Barna Group, OmniPoll 1-14, January-February 2014; N = 945 unchurched adults

notional Christians, adherents of non-Christian faiths, and skeptics.

To be included in the born-again category, people must say they have made a personal commitment to Jesus Christ that is still important in their life today, and believe that when they die they will go to heaven because they have confessed their sins and have accepted Jesus Christ as their Savior.

Evangelicals are those who not only satisfy the born-again criteria but also meet seven other standards that conform to the belief statement of the National Association of Evangelicals.[9] Under Barna Group's rubric, all evangelicals are born again, but not all born-again people are evangelicals (in fact, only about one out of five qualifies). Of course, only God knows who is genuinely born again, so this is not an effort to judge but simply to classify so that ministry leaders can make informed outreach decisions. Similarly, classifying someone as an evangelical is simply a sociological construct; the Bible doesn't use the term. We do *not* classify people as born-again or evangelical Christians because they assign that label to themselves. Our testing of self-classifications has revealed only a weak correlation between self-identification and the theological underpinnings that justify such a label. Overall, only 2 percent of the churchless meet the evangelical criteria, and an additional 14 percent are born again but not evangelical—making a total of 16 percent who are unchurched but born again. We'll look more closely at these folks in the next chapter.

The largest Christian-oriented segment is the "notional" category. These are individuals who identify themselves as

Christians, but do not meet the born-again criteria. They represent almost half of the unchurched: 47 percent.

The remaining segments include people who are aligned with a faith group that is not Christian. These make up 12 percent of the churchless community, comprised of Jews (4 percent), people affiliated with Eastern religions (including Buddhism, Hinduism, Taoism, etc.; 4 percent), Muslims (2 percent), and another percent from other faiths. It is not surprising that the vast majority of people with non-Christian religious allegiances do not attend a church, but it is interesting to note that many also do not attend services or events associated with their faith group. For instance, 61 percent of Jews have not attended a religious event at a synagogue in more than six months. The numbers are even higher for other non-Christian groups: 66 percent of Muslims and

Spiritual Segmentation of the Unchurched

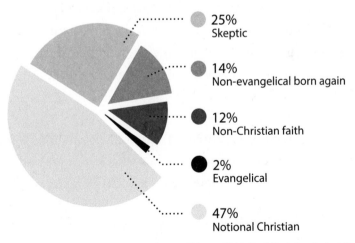

25%
Skeptic

14%
Non-evangelical born again

12%
Non-Christian faith

2%
Evangelical

47%
Notional Christian

Source: Barna Group, OmniPoll 1-14, January-February 2014; N = 945 unchurched adults

68 percent of adults associated with Eastern religions have not attended services or events in their religious community.

The final segment is the skeptics, a group comprised of atheists and agnostics. Their number has increased rapidly in the past few years, especially among adults under thirty. Skeptics represent 25 percent of all unchurched adults in America. Not surprisingly, more than four out of five skeptics qualify as unchurched.

Beliefs about the Bible

Daniel Hahn, pastor of Bible Fellowship Church in Ventura, California, recounted this story:

> I'm preaching through Colossians right now.
> Recently an unchurched 20-something guy who
> was visiting really took me to task on the Scriptural
> exclusivity of Christ. He said, "Well, if Colossians
> teaches that, then that just proves the Bible is false."
> I thought, Wow . . . that's an interesting line of logic.
> Proves the Bible is false? Amazing how far off the
> cliff we've fallen.

The Bible is the bestselling book of all time; it sells so many copies year after year that bestseller lists don't bother to include it. Yet it is more than a book. It is the words, stories, and principles of God preserved for and presented to humans for their best interests and for God's personal glory. The Bible states that God inspired the words written down by the human authors.[10] More documentation supports the veracity of the Bible than exists in support of any other ancient document. Its content has proven to be true over the course of centuries. It is the most studied piece of literature in human history and one of the most widely respected books on the planet.

The unchurched, however, are not overly impressed by the pedigree, history, or importance of the Bible. Yes, as we saw earlier, three-quarters have at least one Bible in their household. Yes, two-thirds consider it to be "sacred literature." But they generally do not consider it unique or trustworthy, and relatively few seek to live in concert with its principles. Less than one out of four unchurched adults firmly believes that the Bible "is totally accurate in all of the principles it teaches." Subgroups most likely to doubt the accuracy of the Bible are younger adults, those with college degrees, those raised in the Catholic church, Asians, and individuals who hold mostly liberal views on social and political matters.

The inerrancy debate does not hold much interest for the unchurched. Only one-eighth believe the Bible contains the actual words of God and should be taken literally, word for word. Another one out of seven views it as the inspired Word of God, containing no errors, but including some passages that are symbolic, not literal. One out of six says the Bible is the inspired Word of God but contains factual and historical errors. One out of ten believes it is not the inspired Word of God, but represents how those who wrote the text understood the ways and principles of God.

The most common perspective among the unchurched (27 percent) is that the Bible is "just another book of teachings written by men that contains stories and advice." Nearly one in ten of the churchless (8 percent) just aren't sure what to make of the Bible.

The churched, not surprisingly, have different views on the Bible. As you can see from the first two responses in the following table, churched adults are much more likely to consider the Bible to be inerrant (72 percent) and therefore trustworthy. As much as anything else, this gap between the two groups may be most responsible for the inability of the churched and unchurched to grasp each other's perspectives.

What Is the Bible?

View of the Bible	Churched	Unchurched
The actual Word of God; it should be taken literally, word for word	33%	12%
The inspired Word of God; it has no errors, although some verses are meant to be symbolic rather than literal	39	17
The inspired Word of God; it has some factual or historical errors	14	17
Not inspired by God but tells how the writers of the Bible understood the ways and principles of God	5	13
Just another book of teachings written by men that contains stories and advice	4	32
Some other view of the Bible	1	2
Not sure	3	8

Source: American Bible Society "State of the Bible," conducted by Barna Group, January 2013 and January 2014; combined sample sizes of 1,897 unchurched and 2,151 churched

The general confusion about how to view the Bible is evident in churchless people's understanding of how it stacks up against the sacred literature of other faiths. When asked if they believe that "the Bible, Koran, and Book of Mormon are all different expressions of the same spiritual truths," 15 percent strongly agreed and 20 percent strongly disagreed. That leaves the bulk of the unchurched—nearly two-thirds—hedging their bets in the middle ground or admitting they do not know.

Beliefs about Faith Priorities

It is perhaps not surprising that the unchurched and the churched have dramatically different ideas about the purpose of life and what should be the central focus of Christian faith.

The churched and churchless differ radically in their responses to a statement about priorities. The statement we posed suggested "the single, most important purpose in life is to love God with all your heart, soul, mind, and strength." That, of course, is taken from Jesus' words recorded in Mark 12:30. Three-quarters of churched people strongly agreed with that statement, while only 39 percent of the unchurched agreed. Men, young adults, college graduates, Asians, liberals, and residents of the blue states were all less likely than the norm to agree.

Unchurched adults had an easier time strongly agreeing with a different statement that gauged their view of Christianity rather than necessarily their personal perspective: "The most important priority of the Christian life is to try hard to be a good and moral person." This time 62 percent of the unchurched bought in, only a few percentage points lower than churched people.

The distance between the unchurched's answers to these statements points us to two possible conclusions. First, the unchurched are not sure what to think about God or how to act toward him. Assenting that loving him is the highest purpose of life would force them to admit that he exists and he reigns—and a majority of the unchurched are not yet ready to embrace that position. Second, the unchurched are prone to thinking of religion in general, and Christianity in particular, as a set of rules to be followed. Although authentic Christianity is just the opposite—it is about *being* rather than *doing*, and freedom more than rules—the perceptions, observations, and experience of the unchurched do not align with this understanding of the faith.

Moreover, the fact that more than three out of every five churchgoing Christians equate Christianity with a list of moral rules to be followed is troubling—especially the fact that they agreed this is "the most important" priority of following Jesus. This flies in the face of Christian teaching that says our ability to follow rules is not what makes us righteous before God (see Romans 4:5 or Ephesians 2:8-9). It is fascinating that there is so little distinction between the churched and churchless on this question. As we will see in chapter 14, millions of Christians embrace self-righteous attitudes and embody legalistic actions. This reminds us that even as we worry about the *un*righteousness in society, we have to concern ourselves with *self*-righteousness inside the church.

Reflections on Foundational Beliefs

To many unchurched people, attending a church looks like becoming an active participant in a club or organization whose central purpose is to celebrate and promote a leader who has never visited the group and is not alive; that is based on a life philosophy that was written thousands of years ago in a very different culture; and whose core values are often misunderstood or even ignored by other members. How difficult, with these assumptions, to see how belonging to a local church is desirable or even reasonable.

Christians base their faith and related behaviors on the Bible. Many unchurched people view the Bible like any other book of stories or self-help they can order from Amazon. Because they lack trust in the reliability and authenticity of Scripture, there is not much chance they will adopt its words as absolute truth. They may appreciate some of its best-known content—the Golden Rule or some of the Ten Commandments, for instance—but most are far from convinced that, taken together, it is a life-guiding and transformational word from God.

Churchless adults tend to struggle with the reality of the supernatural. They are not prepared to worship a God they are not sure exists, commit to a Savior they are not convinced they need, or seek guidance from a Spirit they believe is a literary symbol. Churchgoers may argue that attending a church would personally introduce the churchless to the persons of the Trinity, but most unchurched people have "been there, done that" and walked away unconvinced. They generally do not believe that God is in the trenches with us, feeling our pain and sharing our suffering. Most call the shots for their own life, and they alone deal with the consequences. They are generally not thankful for what Christ accomplished on the cross because most do not view themselves as sinners in need of a Savior. They may accept God as the Creator of the universe, but many do not give him credit for much since then, and most do not reflect on what his presence means for their lives. If they believe that God exists, the unchurched are more likely to embrace a deistic vision of a god who no longer interacts with his creation.

Most unchurched adults are not troubled by the battle between good and evil, ignoring the possibility that they may be actors in an ongoing struggle for which the chief prize is their soul. They are not worried about the destructive ways of the devil because they don't believe he exists. Those who do believe there is a devil do not worry about what he is up to, confident in their abilities to resist and in some undefined but benevolent force that is certainly on their side.

The foundational beliefs espoused by most born-again Christians seem nonsensical or outlandish to many unchurched people. As a result, Sunday morning seems like a pretty good time to sleep in rather than participate in the rituals of a group that believes in all these spiritual theories. The idea that spiritual forces are seeking their engagement in a battle just doesn't seem believable. They have had lots of exposure to the teachings, traditions, rituals, and people connected to church-based Christianity, but what they have

THE CREED OF THE CREEDLESS

experienced has not connected spiritual realities to their
everyday existence.

 Forward Thinking

- Among the unchurched people you know, what is the
  foundational Christian belief that seems hardest to accept?
  Why do you think that is?
- Why do you think so many unchurched people understand
  Christianity as a works-based religious system? Why do you
  think so many churchgoers think of Christianity this way?
- Many unchurched people are unmoved when churched people
  appeal to the Bible as the final word on matters of faith.
  How can you find common ground for conversations with
  unchurched people?

1 in 6 unchurched Americans is a born-again Christian.*
That's 18 million people.

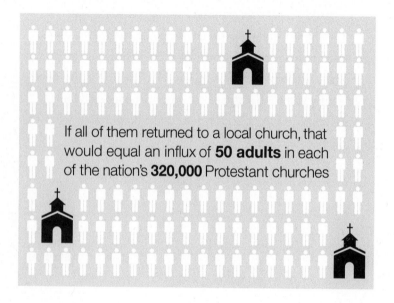

If all of them returned to a local church, that would equal an influx of **50 adults** in each of the nation's **320,000** Protestant churches

Born-again Christians have made a personal commitment that is important in their life today and believe they will go to heaven because they have confessed their sins and accepted Christ as their Savior

Get full color infographics from this book at www.barna.org/churchless

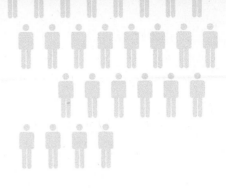

7

BORN AGAIN AND UNCHURCHED

The Paradox of Trusting Christ but Not the Local Church

The first time George showed a colleague the draft of an article he'd written that included a paragraph about the substantial number of unchurched born-again adults, the colleague returned the document with that paragraph circled in red. "I'm sure glad you had me read this," he said, smiling. "Boy, would you be embarrassed if this ever got printed." When George told him the information was accurate, he stared in shock. "Oh," he finally said, and walked away.

Many people have a similar reaction when they learn that one out of six unchurched adults is born again. We have encountered pastors who hear this statistic and argue it's just not possible both to rely on Jesus for eternal grace *and* to intentionally avoid involvement in a local church. Yet many of these ardent believers have chosen to disassociate from a church they believe is too different from the family of faith they see in the Bible. (In chapter 8 we'll look more closely at reasons why these born-again believers and other de-churched individuals have left the church.) Their salvation is firmly intact and is unrelated to their church attendance, despite the fact that many churches and church leaders act as if those two issues are inextricably joined.

Not a New Pattern

For twenty-plus years, Barna Group has tracked the church engagement of churchless adults who meet the born-again criteria we use in our studies. The growth of their numbers has gathered momentum in recent years. Two decades ago, just 8 percent of born-again Christians did not attend church. Since then, the figure has doubled to 16 percent.

Born-again adults—again, a classification based not on self-identification but on their having made a personal commitment to Jesus Christ that is important in their life, and believing that they will go to heaven because they have confessed their sins and accepted Christ as their Savior— constitute a group of about 18 million people. If all of them returned to the local church in the next five years, the influx would represent the largest immigration into Christian churches during any five-year period in US history. Looked at differently, if those believers returned and were spread evenly across the nation's 320,000 or so conventional

Protestant churches, every congregation would grow by an average of more than fifty adults. Since the median size of congregations is slightly more than one hundred adults, most churches would grow by almost half their current size.

While the return of the entire group is improbable, the return of a sizeable number of them is not. Compared to other churchless adults, the born-again subgroup is considerably more open to reconnecting with a church family. Consider this comparison between the two portions of the unchurched universe.

Compared to the non-born-again unchurched, those who are both churchless and born again are more likely to:

- Strongly agree that the Bible is totally accurate in all the principles it teaches (44 percent v. 9 percent)

- Strongly affirm that their religious faith is very important in their life today (66 percent v. 20 percent)

- Strongly disagree that Jesus committed sins while he was on earth (44 percent v. 16 percent)

- Possess an orthodox, biblical view of the nature of God (88 percent v. 33 percent)

- Have prayed to God during the past seven days (95 percent v. 43 percent)

- Have read from the Bible during the past seven days (34 percent v. 6 percent)

- Consider the Bible to be without errors (71 percent v. 16 percent)

- Read the Bible at least once a month (37 percent v. 9 percent)

- Own a Bible (98 percent v. 74 percent)

- Have a very favorable impression of Christianity (60 percent v. 18 percent)

This profile does not mean de-churched born agains are looking for a church home, but it does suggest that of all the segments within the unchurched population, this subgroup is most likely to consider returning to regular church engagement.

Reflections on Churchless Born Agains

According to our data, born-again unchurched people are most likely to return to church through a discussion in their home with a trusted church leader; by attending a high-quality concert or seminar sponsored by the church; or in response to a pastor's sermon(s) on CD or podcast heard prior to visiting a church. They are most likely to consider a church that has a reputation for helping the poor in the community and for providing hands-on, realistic counsel and assistance to young people.

Most unchurched born agains lean toward connecting with a small or midsized congregation—but they usually return to a large church. The most common reason for this paradoxical behavior is that large churches are more likely to engage in outreach efforts like those described above. In addition, most born-again churchless people are seeking a broad range of outreach and in-reach ministry options.

Be warned: Churchless born agains are not interested in being pressured into immediate engagement. They left the fold before, and they will do it again if they feel they are being manipulated to participate in programs or activities merely to help an organization reach its quantitative goals. If they return, it will be for spiritual and relational reasons; they do not want to be numbers on the bottom line or cogs in the machine.

 ## Forward Thinking

- Before reading this chapter, were you aware of the large number of born-again unchurched people in America? Do you know any churchless born-again Christians? If so, what are their reasons for staying disengaged from the church?
- Imagine you are an unchurched born-again Christian. What would you find appealing about your faith community? What might deter you from visiting or getting involved?
- What does your church need to do differently to connect with churchless born agains? What are the obstacles? How will you overcome them?

A Journey Away

Among young adults with a Christian background...

Exiles

2 in 10

Feeling lost between church culture and the wider culture, these young Christians are still active in their faith but tend to ask a lot of questions as they work to apply their faith in a changing, complex world.

Nomads

While they still consider themselves Christians at this stage, young adults' church engagement level has dropped dramatically as they explore other worldviews, lifestyles, and pathways.

4 in 10

Prodigals

11 %

This group of previously churched young adults has dropped out altogether and no longer accepts the Christian faith.

Get full color infographics from this book at www.barna.org/churchless

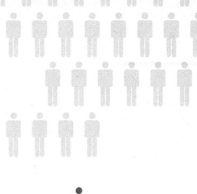

8

DISENGAGED AND DROPPING OUT

Understanding the Reasons People Choose to Leave Church Life

The fact that most unchurched adults fall in the de-churched camp rather than in the purely unchurched category means we need to try to understand people's reasons for leaving church. Most faith communities place a high priority on the number of people involved in their ministry, viewing it as a gauge of success, so the "dropout problem" is quite meaningful (alarming!) to many churches. But the issue is more nuanced than many churchgoing Christians assume. The challenge is to understand the unique reasons people disconnect from churches on their spiritual journey. Some depart from church life due to a felt need for more extensive spiritual exploration; others to redefine the space where the culture and their faith intersect; still others in outright rejection of the Christian faith they once pursued. Effective outreach to these various groups cannot be one-size-fits-all.

No single reason explains why most currently unchurched people have left the church. Most of our significant life decisions are driven by a confluence of factors that combine to push us over the edge into a new behavior. Considering the fragmented lifestyles common to today's culture, especially among young adults, the discovery that there are many reasons for leaving churches behind should not come as a shock.

Many of Barna Group's resources and energies have been devoted to understanding the departure of young adults from church life when they leave home for college or enter the workforce after high school or college. Since the publication of *You Lost Me* in 2011,[11] we have heard from hundreds of people in older generations who saw themselves in one of the three typical dropout journeys David identified in that book: the nomads, the exiles, and the prodigals. While most of our research centered on young adults, we've discovered that much of it is accurate for older adults as well. Since each de-churched person's reasons for dropping out are unique, understanding these different patterns can help us avoid pigeonholing dropouts of any age.

Of the three categories, _nomads_ are the most common. Four out of every ten young adults who were church regulars as teens fall into this category. These are young adults who reflect the zeitgeist of their generation, trying on every worldview, lifestyle, and pathway that is open to them, majoring on experiences and relationships rather than on truth and restraint. They are flexing their independence in multiple dimensions of life and challenging the value and purpose of virtually every institution they encounter: church, family, government, civic organizations, and so forth. They still call themselves Christians and have generally positive views about the Christian faith, but their engagement level has dropped dramatically and their sense of belonging to a specific, organized faith community has all but evaporated.

Roughly one out of every five young adults is an *exile* who feels lost between church culture and the wider culture he or she feels called to inhabit and influence. Exiles are not anti-Christian or even necessarily anti-church; they are simply individuals who do not fit the typical molds that churches expect or support. They are characterized by wanting to follow Jesus while at the same time authentically connecting with their world. They do not want to make life an either/or scenario: either they march in lockstep with the church or they embrace everything the world has to offer at the expense of their faith. Exiles want to be obedient to God *and* be accepted and influential in the wider cultural marketplace. In their eyes, churches often make this exceptionally hard. Exiles tend to ask a lot of questions, as they try to figure out how to apply their faith in a changing, complex culture. In this regard, being an exile is not a negative reality for most of these young adults. They want their faith to matter in the world, and they won't settle for platitudes or superficial expressions of spirituality.

The least common scenario—affecting one out of every

nine young people with a Christian background—is the journey of the *prodigals*, those who drop out of the church because they no longer accept Christianity. Research indicates that a small minority of prodigals may return to the faith and to church life in the future, but it will likely be a matter of years, rather than weeks or months, before they consider returning to a community of Christian faith.

Churches and Young Adults

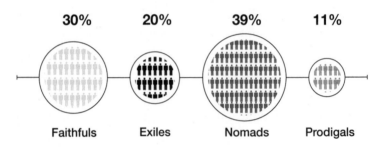

30%	20%	39%	11%
Faithfuls	Exiles	Nomads	Prodigals

For young people to drop out of church life is now normal, though it is not inevitable. Tens of millions of young Christians begin attending church during their preschool, elementary, or high school years and never lose their faith or drop out of church. (In the graphic above, these young people are labeled "Faithfuls," because they have thus far stayed in the flow of congregational life.) Leaving church is always a possibility but never a forgone conclusion.

One of the interesting patterns in the data is a progression through each faith journey. Granted, as the wisdom of Jesus' parable of the sower reveals (see Matthew 13 and Mark 4), people's faith progresses in different ways and with divergent outcomes, depending on many factors that soften or harden their spirit toward God. But a common progression to becoming a prodigal happens like this:

- Faithful young adults trying to find their way to a livable, holistic faith take a typical first step toward de-conversion by becoming an exile. If they are unable to reconcile their doubts and questions, they are likely to progress to the next stage in their walk away from church: that of the nomads.

- Not all nomads begin as exiles; some simply lapse from regular church engagement through apathy or shifting priorities. But when the Christian community does not provide a thoughtful or challenging response to their deeper probing, exiles often lose interest in and passion for the things of God and adopt a nomadic apathy.

- The last step of the de-conversion process is to become a prodigal, an ex-Christian. Not only have these individuals left the church but they have also given up their faith in Christ. Being a prodigal is the rarest of the outcomes—but it happens often enough to break the hearts of parents and pastors.

The point is that prodigals often begin their progression away from Christianity as exiles—fervent followers of Christ who feel caught between church and culture. How can we do a better job of helping young exiles, who are at a crucial junction on their faith journey? A good place to start is by creating an honest and safe place for people to wrestle with doubts and questions, so they can discover for themselves—while still remaining connected to the Christian community—that historic Christianity offers compelling answers to life's most important issues. It might mean admitting that we have too often given young people a simplistic version of the Good News, that at times we have reduced following Jesus to praying a prayer and joining a church.

The exile experience is not unique to Mosaics, the teens and twentysomethings of today. While leaving church has not always been the norm for young adults, it seems to have started in force with the Boomer generation, who put their unique stamp on the Christian journey as they came of age. Surveys from the first half of the 1900s indicate that young adults then were just as likely as their elders to attend church. In the 1960s, however, the generations began to diverge: Boomers, who changed everything about what was normal life in America, are the first generation to have abandoned church life upon reaching their "freedom years." Influenced by a variety of world events and cultural factors, Boomers opened a Pandora's box; subsequent generations have not only followed their lead but taken their novel behaviors further. The dropout problem we have today is the natural fruit of the seeds planted and nurtured by the Boomers as they came of age.

Combine access to information that challenges the

development of a commonly accepted worldview; individual empowerment to embrace various lifestyles and relationships; alienation from institutions that have traditionally formed the foundation of society; and skepticism toward sources of authority—and you get the complex engine that is driving the dropout problem among young adults. The reasons twentysomethings offer for disconnecting from church are informed by these cultural realities, which are most pronounced among Mosaics. But they are also reasons that resonate with older believers as well, as we have discovered since *You Lost Me* was published. Let's take a closer look at the perspectives on church offered by twentysomething dropouts, and use these as a lens through which to see de-churched adults more clearly.

Why Young Adults Drop Out

A majority of young Christians disconnect from church life as young adults, either permanently or for a prolonged period of time. These are the six main reasons young Christians give for leaving church.

1. Churches seem restrictive and overprotective.

Self-expression has become one of the foundations of our postmodern culture. There is less concern about truth than about freedom to express feelings, ideas, and experiences. The demand for expressive liberty has certainly threaded its way into the realm of spirituality, as well—which poses a problem for many churches, since many young adults say their experience of church feels stifling, fear-based, and risk-averse.

Among the previously churched, one out of four adults under thirty (23 percent) indicates that "Christians demonize everything outside of the church." Similar statements are that churches ignore the problems of the real world (22 percent) and that the priorities of Christians are off base, with 18 percent specifically noting that their congregation was "too concerned that movies, music, and video games are harmful." For a group of people who have replaced judgment with tolerance, the perception that the church restricts expression while turning a blind eye to real-world problems leads to a view of the church as, at best, an ineffective organization—and, at worst, a hypocritical one.

2. Christianity as practiced is too shallow.

Today's young adults are the most overstimulated and widely educated generation in American history. They are constantly bombarded by information, images, sounds, and choices, and most are not content with a consistently ho-hum experience from church or anywhere else. For many, neither the local church as an institution nor the communal church as a relational entity is sufficiently unique or necessary to compel their involvement.

Millions of young dropouts agree that something was lacking in their church experience. One-third (31 percent) say "church is boring." One-quarter (24 percent) note that "faith is not relevant to my career or interests," showing their dissatisfaction with a non-integrated Christianity. One out of four

(23 percent) chides the local church for inadequate teaching, claiming that "the Bible is not taught clearly or often enough." Most concerning is the one-fifth (20 percent) of young dropouts who admit "God seems missing from my experience of church." We'll talk more about this perception—and how it affects the churchless—in the final chapter.

The disheartening reality of their disappointment is that these are not people clamoring for graduate-level theology or biblical studies. They are practical-minded young adults trying to make their way through the blizzard of life options and myriad worldviews they encounter. The competitive views offered in the marketplace of ideas are often communicated with more clarity, passion, and applicability than the teaching and worldview formation young people have received from their churches. Many feel as if they have no choice but to seek an alternative.

3. Churches seem antagonistic to science.

Christianity and science have been at loggerheads for centuries. The specific scientific discoveries and theories at issue these days may be new, but the tension between the two systems of explaining life is not. However, for many young adults the increased intensity of the conflict is counterproductive and a source of cognitive dissonance.

Many young dropouts are not science apologists as much as they are students seeking an honest conversation about reality. Consequently, more than one-third of twentysomething dropouts (35 percent) believe that "Christians are too confident they know all the answers." Nearly as many (29 percent) contend that "churches are out of step with the scientific world we live in." One out of four (25 percent) says that "Christianity is antiscience" and a similar proportion (23 percent) say they are "turned off by the creation-versus-evolution debate." Our research also found that many science-minded young Christians are struggling to find ways of staying faithful to both their religious beliefs and their sense of professional calling into a science-related field.

4. Churches are judgmental and rigid about sexuality.

These days we see little restraint when it comes to public displays of sexually charged content. Digital pornography, sexualized children and teenagers, the widespread acceptance of multiple sexual partners and orientations—these characterize our current era as one of sexual promiscuity, experimentation, and sharing. Growing up in such an environment has left young people struggling with how to live meaningful lives in terms of sex and sexuality.

Perhaps even more than young people, churches are flummoxed about how to respond. The traditional emphases on sexual purity and waiting for marriage to become sexually active seem increasingly outdated to the broader culture, but some in the Christian community are beginning to wonder if the problem has more to do with how churches express these positions than with the standards themselves. Interwoven with these issues are other cultural shifts such as delayed marriage, tens of millions of births outside marriage, and the relaxation of sexual regulations in the media. Many churches do not know how to respond with both truth and love to these sweeping changes.

Most Christian young adults are as sexually active as their non-Christian peers, even though they are more conservative in their attitudes about sexuality. One out of six young Christians say they "have made mistakes and feel judged in church because of them." Sexual issues are especially important among young Catholics. Within that segment, two-fifths (40 percent) agree the Catholic church's "teachings on sexuality and birth control are out of date."

5. The exclusivity of Christianity is a turnoff.

A hallmark value of modern society is the ability to choose one's beliefs in a manner that is personally satisfying and unique. Sociologists have hailed today's young adults as the most eclectic generation in American history in terms of race, ethnicity, sexuality, religion, technological tools, and sources of authority. Young adults typically embrace tolerance, open-mindedness, flexibility, and inclusiveness, and most want to find areas of common ground with each other, even if that requires minimizing real and critical differences.

In this context, Christianity's claims that Jesus is the only way to salvation, that the Bible is the only reliable and authoritative word of God, and that Christianity is the only faith that connects people to the Creator and Ruler of the universe upset many young adults. Three out of ten (29 percent) young dropouts say "churches are afraid of the beliefs of other faiths," and an identical proportion feel they are "forced to choose between my faith and my friends." One-fifth (22 percent) say "church is like a country club, only for insiders."

6. Churches are unfriendly to those who doubt.

Many young adults who formerly attended a Christian church feel that churches are not safe places to wrestle with doubts about the beliefs, teachings, or practices of Christianity. Admitting that some aspects of the Christian faith do not make sense to them puts them at risk of alienation from their faith community. Even when that doesn't occur, many young dropouts feel the church's responses to their doubt are superficial or even insulting to their intelligence.

More than one-third (36 percent) of young dropouts say they are unable "to ask my most pressing life questions in church" while one-quarter (23 percent) indicate they have "significant intellectual doubts about my faith." Even when their doubts do not directly relate to faith issues, a significant number of young unchurched adults (18 percent) feel misunderstood and ignored in times of need because churches "do not help with depression or other emotional problems."

The Necessity of a New Approach

Most churches divide their ministries into a series of lifestyle groups designed to address the needs of a particular demographic. Ministries cater to the needs of young suburban professionals, comfortably retired executives, struggling single moms, dual-income parents, upwardly mobile newly married thirtysomethings—identify any target group and you'll find a church or ministry focused on reaching out to that segment.

Engaging the churchless population has traditionally been handled the same way: define a "typical" church dropout and develop a ministry solution for that crowd. However, the diversity within the cohort of young church dropouts poses a challenge to that tried-and-true method. Two decades ago you could identify a handful of common motives underlying the departure of young adults from church engagement. Today, however, the dropout population is far more individualized, making single-solution, one-size-fits-all ministry efforts less and less effective.

The issues young people face are myriad and challenging. Their lifestyles are incredibly diverse. Their religious beliefs and expectations are hard to nail down. Their support systems are hybrid and unpredictable. And their long-term plans either don't exist or change with astonishing frequency. The life journeys of today's young adult dropouts are being delayed, reordered, redefined, and sometimes upended altogether—and many churches that rely on traditional life-formation patterns are finding fewer people involved and less success transforming those lives. The traditional family path has been replaced by a new normal that is not normal at all by traditional standards, as we'll explore in the next chapter. Trying to figure out and implement the best way to come alongside young adults with support and effective discipleship is like trying to hit a moving target.

Some in the church protest that young people will return to church life "just like they always do"—when they have kids. Having children, they say, is one of the surest ways for young Americans to be introduced to the value of a local faith community. However, recent sociological trends give us good reason to doubt the reliability of this assumption. Mosaics are less likely to marry than previous generations, and those who do marry head to the altar an average of six years later than the Boomers and Busters who preceded them. They are more likely to have children outside of a marital relationship, and those who have children tend to start their family later in life. This group of young people is eight times more likely than young people raised in the 1960s to come from homes where their biological parents were never married.

Even if young adults are driven back to church by marriage and family—and that assumption is highly questionable—they will return in a much different life space than prior generations were when they came back to the fold. They are likely to be older, if and when they return. They will come back with different emotional, financial, spiritual, and relational needs due to a wealth of experiences that have no parallel in prior generations. They will practice family in new ways. How will churches support and disciple the "new normal" family?

And that's *if* they return. According to our studies, fully half of today's young parents report that having children did *not* influence their desire or effort to connect to a church. (This perspective is most common among skeptic parents who are atheists or agnostics; nine out of ten say becoming a parent had no influence on their likelihood to connect with a faith community.) Even among parents who are born-again

Christians, nearly half (47 percent) say that having children did not impact their churchgoing habits.

We cannot expect to be effective by merely "modernizing" the approaches churches have long relied on to attract and retain young families.

Reflections on Dropouts

While real generational differences exist between Mosaic and older adult dropouts, twentysomethings' reasons for disconnecting from church life cross generational lines. Churches that are unwelcoming to young adults' doubts and questions are equally unwelcoming to older adults' doubts and questions—and many have both! Likewise, many older adults, like Mosaics, find their church experience to be shallow and disconnected from their everyday lives. We have heard again and again from Buster, Boomer, and even Elder adults who see themselves reflected in the nomad, exile, or prodigal faith journeys, and who struggle to determine what church involvement means for them.

These new times require new strategies for making faith real in people's lives. Nothing drives home the need for such innovation as attempting to connect (or reconnect) with the de-churched. Their dismissal of Christian churches is not mean-spirited; it simply reflects the firsthand experiences that led them to conclude churches are ill-equipped to support the flourishing life they hope for.

Among most dropouts, honesty and authenticity are hallmarks of this hoped-for life. Yet if we are honest with ourselves, authenticity is not always a characteristic of church life. How well do we teach, disciple, and counsel with kindness, honest self-disclosure, and a willingness to speak truth without condemnation? We approach others out of self-righteousness rather than out of an honest admission that we, too, need a Savior. Let's listen with open minds to the criticisms offered by dropouts of every age. We may discover how we have missed the mark in our attempts to serve God and expand his Kingdom, and thus change and grow into the church God intends for us to be.

Waiting patiently for dropouts to arrive at some magical life event that will bring them back to church is a fool's game. While parenthood, midlife crises, job loss, financial difficulty, and retirement are all seasons that can clarify and enhance spiritual pursuits, there is no guarantee that any of these inevitably lead to church engagement. It is up to faith communities to communicate with dropouts and other unchurched folks about how church involvement can meet their felt spiritual needs and imbue their lives with meaning and significance. Life transitions alone will not be enough to convince them.

Likewise, effectively incorporating a diversity of people into congregational life will demand greater flexibility and creativity on the part of faith communities. Ministry strategies and discipleship programs that were successful in the past may need to be reimagined or even scrapped for something new. Rather than spawning ever-more-segmented ministries that further silo various demographics, what would it look like if churches started with the premise that godly relationships nurtured over the long haul can transcend the science of demography? What if churches prioritized seeking and finding God together over activities and events designed to appeal to ever-shrinking slices of their constituency?

Because, more than anything else, churches have to deliver the goods. One thing we hear from churchless and churched people alike is that they intensely desire the local church to provide what no other group can offer: an experience of the presence of God. Why should they go to a church if there's no evidence God is there? When former church regulars say they are more likely to return to church if they have reason to believe God is present and active in a congregation, we can assume they couldn't find him when they used to attend. Can you blame these folks for not showing up when the Guest of Honor is not ushered into the hall?

 ## Forward Thinking

- Have you encountered dropouts whose spiritual journeys track with the patterns of nomads, exiles, or prodigals? In your experience, what do these folks have in common? What experiences or attitudes make their journeys unique?

- Which of the six perspectives on church offered by young dropouts seems most likely to be true of your faith community? Why and in what ways?

- Which of your ministry strategies or discipleship programs is most in need of reevaluation in light of new cultural realities facing the church? How will you address the challenges?

46% of the unchurched say family is their highest priority...

But what does family look like to them?

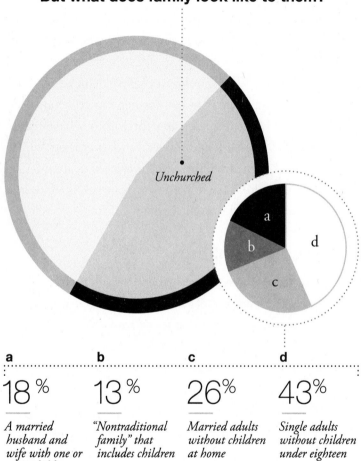

Unchurched

a
....

a

18%

A married husband and wife with one or more children under eighteen

b

13%

"Nontraditional family" that includes children

c

26%

Married adults without children at home

d

43%

Single adults without children under eighteen

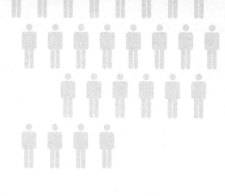

9

THE INTERSECTION OF FAMILY AND FAITH

Family Life among Unchurched People

As pop-culture powerhouses like *Modern Family*, *Real Housewives*, and *New Girl* reveal, the American family is being reinvented. Some distinctive norms certainly differentiate the average churchgoing family from the average unchurched family, but the unconventional is becoming more normal across both segments of American family life. More blended families. More single parents sharing the kids on alternate weekends. More gay and lesbian couples raising children. More twenty- and thirtysomething singles forming de facto households. More diverse ideas about what family means.

The Mosaics are accelerating the reinvention of family

that has been underway for forty years. Young adults are the most pragmatic generation yet when it comes to marriage; while most want to get married (someday), it's got to "work" for them. Same with raising children—before most other considerations, Mosaics look at the practical issues involved in starting a family. And if those reinventions aren't enough, many young adults are redefining "family" to include their tribe of friends.

But the overhaul of the American family doesn't end (or begin) with young adults. Think about even the most conventional, *Leave It to Beaver*-ish family unit. That father, mother, 2.5 kids, and a dog—whether or not they attend church—are under enormous pressures of activity, busyness, and distraction. Between youth sports leagues, school-based programs, and extracurricular activities, many kids (and their minivan-driving parents) are on the go seven days a week. Add in Mom's online class to finish a degree and Dad's out-of-state travel for work, and you've got intense competition for that family's time and engagement.

Church involvement often loses out.

Many churchgoing families are becoming *less* churched simply by virtue of their busy schedules and conflicting demands. The typical rhythm of being a family—even a good Christian family—is becoming less connected to church engagement. Two decades ago a "regular church-goer" was a person who attended at least three weekends per month and often several times per week. But today a regular churchgoer shows up for worship once every four to six weeks. The insanely busy family schedule is creating a whole new species of well-meaning but less-committed churchgoers. They are *almost* churchless, not because they intend to be, but because church involvement is one among dozens of demands.

Most candid church leaders will admit that churchgoing is geared toward conventional families; that is, most churches' "market" is married parents raising children together. But what has been the norm—the conventional family—is becoming less and less so. The orientation of church programming toward a shrinking family demographic will prove to be a challenge for many faith communities because they don't (yet) know how to disciple the rapidly growing number of unconventional—unmarried, overcommitted, nontraditional—families.

Obviously, this lack of preparation has profound implications for the choices we make about ministry, which we will discuss in the final chapter.

The Family Life of the Churchless

Nearly half of churchless people (46 percent) say family is their highest priority. But what does that mean? Something different, perhaps, than what you might expect. A majority of the unchurched (56 percent) are single, whereas a majority of churched people are married (55 percent). In fact, the unchurched are nearly twice as likely as the churched to never have been married, and twice as likely to cohabit. Most of the nation's unchurched adults are not only churchless but also spouseless.

So why and how is family such a big priority for so many of them?

Like most other Americans, the unchurched see family as a network of relationships that provides personal support, security, belonging, purpose, comfort, and the opportunity to receive and give love. They look upon family as a natural part of a normal life, and these relationships represent a vital part of their identity. They know who they are because of their family connections and shared experiences.

But that does not mean the families of the churchless mirror those of churched adults. Three out of every ten unchurched adults have children under the age of eighteen living with them. Most of these young people are in homes with two married parents, but one-fifth are in homes with a single parent who has never been married. One-seventh are in homes with cohabiting adults and a similar number are in homes with parents who are separated or divorced.

Less than one out of every five unchurched households (18 percent) is a "traditional family"—that is, a married husband and wife with one or more children under eighteen.[12] Thirteen percent are "nontraditional families" that include children. One-quarter (26 percent) are married adults without children in the home, while the remaining 43 percent are single adults living without children under eighteen.

Understanding these demographics can help to explain why many of the common approaches to attracting the unchurched—many of which revolve around children—fail to produce the hoped-for results.

Households of the Unchurched

Married with children under 18

18%

Married with no children under 18

26%

Single, never been married, with children under 18

6%

Single, never been married, with no children under 18

23%

Single, living with opposite-sex adult, with children under 18

4%

Single, living with opposite-sex adult, with no children under 18

7%

Divorced with children under 18

2%

Divorced with no children under 18

7%

Separated with children under 18

1%

Separated with no children under 18

1%

Widowed with children under 18

<1%

Widowed with no children under 18

5%

Married with (or without) Children

Unchurched people who are married take their commitment
seriously. The vast majority also claim to be happily married. Three-quarters say one of their highest goals is to stay
married to the same partner for life. (A large share of those
who do not have this goal are single and have no plans to
marry.) Two-thirds say one of their highest goals is to have a
satisfying sex life with their spouse, while half say that having
children is one of their highest goals.

The interest in having children is considerably lower than
among the churched (71 percent) and is related to the fact
that the unchurched are younger—and today's young adults,
churched or not, are less enthusiastic about raising children.
As the costs and complexity of child rearing have increased,
surveys over the past decade have shown declining interest
in raising kids. This shift in attitude may also be related to
the increase in self-centeredness that studies have identified
among churched and churchless young adults. It's the "selfie"
generation—a cohort of young adults who are perfectly comfortable posing for pictures and being the center of attention
on their social media feeds. It's tempting to blame Mosaics
for their narcissistic tendencies, but we have to ask: who
raised this generation? In many ways Mosaics are simply following the Boomers and taking the self-centered revolution
to its logical conclusion. When the question is, *What's in it
for me?*, the self-sacrifice demanded by parenthood is not an
attractive answer.

Still, the churchless are looking for relational connections in this rising tide of entitlement. Nearly half of all unchurched adults agree that having a mentor to coach them through the child-rearing years is very important. However, while millions of them see value in and hope to have a good parenting mentor, relatively few (15 percent) believe they need more parenting input from their peers. Parenting advice offered by friends, neighbors, and associates has little impact and is rarely appreciated.

One of the challenges facing unchurched parents is setting standards and guidelines for teaching their kids right from wrong. In contrast to churched adults, they lack one critical resource: trust in the Bible. Whereas four out of ten churched parents (41 percent) say they rely on the Bible to define moral parameters, only one out of twelve unchurched adults (8 percent) does so. The churchless compensate by trusting their feelings and personal experience to a much greater degree. They are nearly twice as likely as the churched to turn inward for such guidance (77 percent compared to 40 percent). It is interesting to note, however, that when crisis strikes the family, the unchurched and churched report similar responses. They are most likely to turn to their parents (one-third) or their spouse (one-fifth) for help and support. However, 20 percent of churched people say they would also seek out someone connected to their faith, such as a minister or fellow believer, or engage in a spiritual act such as prayer or seeking guidance from the Bible. Only 7 percent of the unchurched would rely on faith resources in a family crisis.

What Churches Bring to the Family Table

Parenting and family life have changed dramatically over the past quarter-century. While the notion of bringing a child to church for religious instruction made sense to parents two and three decades ago, the appeal has fizzled somewhat over time—though it still is stronger than most other motivations the churchless express for coming to church. Today's unchurched parents do not automatically assume that a church can offer them significant help as they raise their children in a confusing and dangerous world. In fact, churchless adults are half as likely as churched parents to believe churches are a very helpful resource for parental development (24 percent versus 47 percent, respectively). We partnered with Reggie Joiner and his organization, Orange,[13] to study how parents, both churched and unchurched, relate to churches and what they expect from church. More than half of churchless parents (54 percent) say they would not seek parenting help from a church.

However, many churchless adults (42 percent) do see churches as an important resource when it comes to the moral, spiritual, and character development of their children. Another 8 percent mention pastors, youth groups, and the Bible as resources of value. In total, half of unchurched adults identify church-related resources as the most helpful tools available to them for shaping the inner life of their children. That's only slightly less than is true among churched adults (58 percent). In the Orange survey, one-quarter of churchless parents (24 percent) said they would like a church to provide support to their family, whether spiritual, emotional, moral, or some other kind. Of all the activities—sports, camps, events—offered by churches to kids and families, what parents want most is help instilling values and character in their children.

Faith-based sports programs provide some success at attracting unchurched families to church-sponsored events. While such programs do not draw a majority of unchurched families, about half feel that a high-quality program would be attractive to them and their children. In particular, however, they are seeking programs that offer facilities, equipment, and training superior to other options available in their community. Only 4 percent say they would be drawn by the provision of spiritual and moral development in conjunction with sports.

Aside from that flicker of interest, however, two-thirds of the churchless say parental training and child-rearing resources and programs would do little or nothing to encourage them to attend a church.

Reflections on Unchurched Family Life

As a review of the last few years' headlines reveals, marriage is being redefined in America. The growing acceptance of same-sex marriage, the acceptance of divorce and serial marriage, the embrace of cohabitation, and increasing skepticism about marriage in general all have an impact on what's considered "normal" when it comes to family. The fact that young adults, in particular, are redefining family to include close friends, even though this is a regularly shifting group, points to the impermanence and unreliability associated with family in the minds of millions of people. Given these continuing shifts, churches may have a difficult time connecting with the unchurched if their ministries are tailored for traditional households. In particular, single and married-without-children adults have little reason to connect with a church if its resources are funneled toward children's and family ministry.

And yet . . . the church must not altogether abandon its ministries to children. As we have documented elsewhere, kids who are exposed to biblical worldview teaching before the age of thirteen are much more likely to pursue Christian faith as an adult than those who are not.[14] Pastor Larry Reichardt of South Coast Fellowship in Ventura, California, emphasizes the importance of connecting with kids where they are, instead of trying to attract them to church first: "We share Christ with kids on the streets and then we visit the kids' families at home and pray for them. We start small groups in their area in English or Spanish and minister to their needs. We also do physical things in the neighborhood to demonstrate we care, sharing the love of God where they are and how they are. Eventually, we ask them to church."

John Burke, cofounder of Gateway Church in Austin, Texas, and president of Emerging Leadership Initiative, points out the worldview differences between today's kids and those who were children decades ago: "I don't see [direct evangelism] as a primary strategy for our post-Christian context. It worked in the '50s through the '80s when the task was clarifying the Gospel of Grace to Builder/Boomer kids who grew up with background knowledge of the God of the Bible and His story. That's no longer the case."

Clearly, the need for churches to introduce kids to God and the Scriptures is as great as ever. But as an ever-greater number of young adults come of age without a foundational understanding of Christian principles and the Bible, churches must also reconsider their strategies for ministering to the unchurched. Does your faith community offer an experience of family to those who are single? Do young marrieds feel incomplete or less than other couples because they don't have children? Are single moms and dads given the kind of support they need to be both parents to their kids? Do divorced folks have a safe place of supportive relationships where they can heal and grow?

As it has for millennia, the church can help families grow in faith and love. To do that, we must adjust our expectations and methods to reflect the changing landscape of the family in our culture.

Forward Thinking

- Do you know the family demographics of your church's surrounding community? How well do your church's ministry priorities reflect those demographics?
- What is your church doing to introduce children to a biblical worldview? How could your kids' ministry be more focused on this goal?
- The modern family comes in many shapes and sizes. To what extent is your faith community "one size fits all" when it comes to family ministry? What could you do to support and nurture families that fall outside the traditional norm?

The most important life goals
among the unchurched

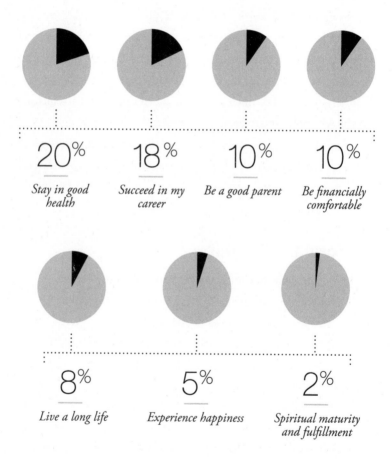

20%
Stay in good health

18%
Succeed in my career

10%
Be a good parent

10%
Be financially comfortable

8%
Live a long life

5%
Experience happiness

2%
Spiritual maturity and fulfillment

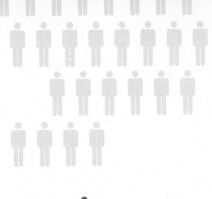

10

THE IDEALS THAT PROPEL THE UNCHURCHED FORWARD

The Goals, Morals, and Values at the Heart of Churchless Adults

If we asked you to identify the single most important goal for your life, what would you say? When we asked a national sample of churchless people, the most popular responses were to experience good health (20 percent) and to succeed in their job or career (18 percent). Other frequently mentioned goals were to do a good job parenting their children (10 percent), to be financially successful or comfortable (10 percent), to live a long life (8 percent), and to experience happiness and fulfillment (5 percent). Only 2 percent listed goals related to faith or spirituality.

These responses are quite similar to those offered by churched adults. The only significant difference is the 12 percent of churched adults who listed a goal related to faith or spirituality. Among churchgoers, faith-related responses were the third-ranked category, marginally higher than parenting and finances. Still, fewer than one in eight churched people identify something related to faith as their top goal in life.

Americans no longer share a common dream. Just one in five Americans hopes to achieve good health, the most common goal for the future. The vast majority of goals maintained by Americans are personal, not communal, a pattern that holds true in responses from churched and unchurched adults alike.

The data presented in the following table provide a glimpse into the differences and similarities between churched and unchurched adults when it comes to ranking their hopes for the future. The results indicate that the churchless desire pretty much the same outcomes as the churched—without involvement in a church or in the Christian faith. They are less interested than churched people in marriage and children and in making a difference in the world, and less worried about grasping their purpose in life—yet purpose, impact, and family are still of significant interest to tens of millions of unchurched people.

Consider the top-ranked outcomes the unchurched desire: Good health. Good friends. A good marriage that provides sexual fulfillment. Integrity. Comfort. Purpose and meaning.

Next, look at the outcomes that are relatively unappealing to them: Pleasure travel. A big house. A high-paying job. The latest technology. Fame. A deep commitment to the Christian faith. Church involvement.

The Life American Adults Hope For

Desired outcomes for their future	Unchurched	Churched
Having good physical health	86%	84%
Living with a high degree of integrity	81	87
Having close personal friendships	73	75
Having a comfortable lifestyle	73	68
Having one marriage partner for life	72	84
Having a clear purpose for living	68	82
Having a satisfying sex life with your marriage partner	65	66
Living close to your family and relatives	56	66
Having children	54	71
Having a close relationship with God	52	86
Making a difference in the world	46	60
Having a college degree	42	48
Working in a high-paying job	30	28
Travelling throughout the world for pleasure	27	29
Being deeply committed to the Christian faith	24	77
Owning a large home	14	21
Being personally active in a church	13	61
Owning the latest household technology and electronics	12	11
Achieving fame or public recognition	7	7

A few outcomes fall within a middle ground—the "waffling zone"—composed of possibilities that do not get them excited, but that might fit into their framework given the right conditions: A dynamic personal relationship with God. Making a difference. Proximity to extended family. Having children. A college education.

When it comes to spiritual goals, those most interested are more often women, people in their fifties and sixties, blacks, born-again Christians, and those who live in red states. A noteworthy exception is the heightened interest in making a difference in the world among unchurched adults who are Hispanic or under the age of thirty.

Morals and Values

Ideologically, the unchurched are different from many who regularly attend church services. This distinctiveness emerges most clearly when we study morals and values.

Any discussion of morals must touch on the basis of those moral choices. For a disciple of Jesus, the Bible is, of course, the standard on which morals are based. But what about those who do not have a biblical foundation upholding their morality? On what basis do they make their moral choices?

Half of the nation's unchurched adults make moral decisions based on their feelings about right and wrong. Another one-third (35 percent) say they do not know what it means for something to be "morally right," so they just do the best they can in whatever situation they find themselves. Nearly one in ten churchless people (9 percent) turns to the Scriptures for moral guidance, while 3 percent rely on current societal standards. Churched people are more likely to rely on the Bible; 39 percent say they use it as their moral compass.

Two in ten unchurched (21 percent) believe absolute moral truth exists, yet just 17 percent of those (which equates to about 4 percent of the entire unchurched segment) believe the Bible is the source of absolute moral truth. A larger proportion would trust parental teaching (36 percent) or personal experiences (27 percent) than would rely on God's Word.

Given their views on the relationship between moral authority and the Bible, it is easier to understand some of the moral stances the unchurched embrace. For instance, when asked about their views on abortion, seven out of ten say abortion should be legal in all (25 percent) or most (45 percent) cases. In contrast, only four in ten churched folks believe abortion should be legal: 11 percent in all cases, 29 percent in most.

Churchless adults are less inclined than the churched to believe that it is important to express their moral views to influence their community. One-third of the unchurched feel such an urge, compared to half of churched adults. Unchurched people are also less likely than churched people to allow their values to influence their media consumption; one-third say their morals and values affect their media exposure a lot, while half of the churched say so.

Reflections on Unchurched Ideals

Many unchurched adults believe that churches are more likely to have a predetermined agenda than to respond to the needs of congregants. Whether or not that perception is accurate, it serves to keep some from attending churches. Knowing what gets the unchurched excited for their future can help churches shape the experiences they offer.

In interactions with the unchurched, church leaders should consider how to downplay connecting with a church and instead emphasize the opportunity to bond with God. The life goals and moral perspectives of the unchurched clearly demonstrate their disinterest in church life—yet they do see value in spiritual depth and direction. A majority continue to believe that a meaningful relationship with God is worthwhile. Focusing on building that bridge is much more important, initially *and* eternally, than signing up another body for the membership count.

There's no question that one of the great distinctives between the Christian life and a more secular approach relates to moral choices. However, churchless people are leery of churches that major on talk about morality and judgment. Certainly we cannot and should not change the essential moral component of the Christian life, but we must be aware that leading with the morality card closes down the conversation immediately. Most unchurched people are simply not interested in reflecting on their morals, reconsidering what is right or wrong, or hearing that there is a definitive source for knowing the difference. If they become followers of Christ, most unchurched adults will have to go through a massive overhaul on these matters, but transformation on that level usually comes in response to a relationship with Christ—not as a prerequisite.

Forward Thinking

- What surprises you most about churchless people's goals and priorities? What surprises you most about churched people's goals and priorities? What do you think could best account for the differences?

- Look again at the top five or six hopes shared by churched and unchurched people, as presented in the table "The Life American Adults Hope For." What is your church community doing to help people make the connection between these goals and a life of faith?

- Is it possible for your church to hold biblical values and morals without compromising, while being open and inviting to unchurched people? How?

Unchurched

Churched

Bottom line: the lifestyles of the churched and
unchurched don't look all that different

Get full color infographics from this book at www.barna.org/churchless

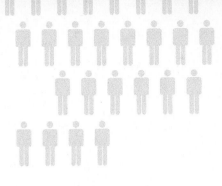

11

THIS IS HOW THEY ROLL

The Lifestyle Choices and Activities of the Unchurched

In this chapter, we will examine the activities and lifestyle choices of unchurched people—but to avoid burying the most significant insight, here's the big headline: There's often not much of a difference between the churched and the churchless when it comes to lifestyle choices. Keep this in mind as we look at how churchless people spend their time.

Our research reveals that the most common activities undertaken by unchurched people—other than eating, sleeping, and working—relate to media use. Like churched adults, the churchless are infatuated with media content, spending more than ten hours each day consuming information from various forms of media. The younger an individual is, the more likely she is to consume input from two or more media sources simultaneously—commonly referred to as "multi-tasking." Because this is such a key area, we'll look at media habits in more detail later in this chapter.

What other activities occupy the time of the churchless? A majority of unchurched people have conversations with other people about things that are meaningful to them. For instance, they are about as likely as churched people to discuss moral issues or situations with others; half (51 percent) had done so during the week prior to their survey interview. And even though they are not church attenders, one-quarter (24 percent) also talked with someone about matters of faith and religious beliefs. That's only a bit less than the proportion of churched adults who did so—though it may be that the conversations differed considerably between the two groups.

Less common but nevertheless widespread activities during a typical week include using profanity in public (39 percent), buying lottery tickets or placing bets (23 percent), and drinking enough alcohol to be considered legally intoxicated (22 percent). The figures for public profanity and drunkenness are notably higher than is found among the churched (23 percent and 7 percent, respectively), but the nearly one-fourth who participated in gambling is close to the same in both camps.

Even fewer members of the churchless population admit to gossiping (13 percent), boycotting products or brands (12 percent), having sexual intercourse or a physical relationship with someone to whom they are not married (11 percent), getting revenge against someone who had hurt or offended them (10 percent), lying (8 percent), or stealing (one percent) in the past week.

Common Activities During the Week

Activity	Unchurched	Churched
Recycled used products/materials	65%	68%
Changed your lifestyle to have a more positive impact on the environment	53	58
Conversation about a specific moral issue or situation	51	57
Used profanity in public	39	23
Intentionally exposed to media that showed explicit or uncensored sexual content	29	16
Conversation about faith with someone who believed differently than you	24	34
Bought a lottery ticket or placed a bet	23	19
Drank enough alcohol to be considered legally drunk or intoxicated	22	7
Gossiped/said mean or untrue things to other people about someone who was not present	13	12
Intentionally boycotted/did not buy a specific product or brand as a protest	12	12
Had an intimate sexual encounter or physical relationship with someone to whom you are not married	11	9
Took actions to take revenge/get back at someone who had hurt or offended you	10	8
Told something to someone that you knew was not the truth	8	13
Stole something that did not belong to you	1	2

Apart from church-related activities and a handful of other behaviors, the unchurched lifestyle is not substantially different from that of churched people. Churchless people tend to live a somewhat "edgier" life—they are more likely to use profanity, get drunk, or view immodest images via the media. But their social interactions—their conversations about faith and morals, and the likelihood of their engaging in behaviors such as gossip, lying, or sexual activity outside of marriage—are all but indistinguishable from churchgoers.

A Closer Look at Media Consumption

Churchless and churched people consume a similar amount of media content in a given day. But do they consume content from the same media? A 2014 study we conducted evaluated how often people use a particular medium to gather new information. In that study, we found that the two groups have a similar media profile as reflected in the following table.

Media Used in a Typical Day

Medium used	Unchurched	Churched
Internet websites	56%	57%
Network television	50	58
Cable television	48	53
Social media	42	36
Mobile/smart phone	41	47
Radio	38	41
Newspapers	24	28
Physical books	14	21
Electronic books	6	6
Magazines	6	10

Source: Barna Group OmniPoll January-February 2014; 297 churched (weekly), 556 unchurched

The two groups are equally likely to subscribe to cable or satellite television service and premium movie channels. In the past year, they watched virtually the same number of movies in a theater; viewed an identical number of televised movies from the comfort of their home; and watched the same number of movies via DVDs, Blu-ray discs, videos, or streaming. Even the number of movies watched in each category of MPAA ratings was nearly identical.

The unchurched emerged as more likely to view media they know contains explicit or uncensored sexual content. Three out of every ten churchless people (29 percent) said that in the past week they had intentionally viewed explicit or uncensored sexual content, compared to about one in six of the churched (16 percent).

Further, we learned that churched adults are somewhat more likely to filter media content to reduce the amount of objectionable material they see. About half of the churched, compared to one-third of the unchurched, said that in the previous week they had turned off a television program because it contained values, morals, or points of view they did not appreciate. Similarly, we discovered that churched people were nearly twice as likely as the unchurched (26 percent versus 14 percent, respectively) to choose not to watch a particular movie solely because the rating for the film indicated that it contained objectionable material.

Overall, then, the choice of media, the frequency of use, and how much time is devoted to media consumption varies little between the two groups. There are, however, slight differences in the content each group is willing to accept.

Self-Improvement and Sacrifice

When it comes to lifestyle choices, what most distinguishes the unchurched from the churched relates to self-improvement and personal sacrifice. These groups approach personal enhancement differently, and the unchurched are notably less willing to sacrifice their resources for the good of others.

Self-Improvement Efforts

Activity done for self-improvement	Unchurched	Churched
Obey the Ten Commandments	31%	20%
Admit I cannot do it alone, need God's help	23	26
Get advice or help from others I trust/respect	15	16
Implement New Year's resolutions	11	7
Force/train self to think/act differently	8	9
Follow the rules/guidelines/advice in the Bible	5	15
Consult media sources (book, website, etc.) for help, insight, or steps toward change	2	4

Most Americans claim they make an effort to improve themselves. How? That's where it gets interesting. While the two segments reflect surprisingly similar strategies for personal growth, the most common strategy employed by the unchurched is trying harder to obey the Ten Commandments. This approach was named by one-third of the churchless (31 percent) . . . and by just one-fifth of the churched (20 percent)! The churched (15 percent) were more likely than the unchurched (5 percent) to improve themselves by trying to follow the rules in the Bible, but one-quarter of each group said they seek self-improvement by asking God to help them grow.

Six out of ten unchurched people gave some type of spiritual response when we asked them about the foundation for their self-improvement efforts. A similar proportion of churched adults offered a spiritually based answer, but their responses were distributed a bit differently.

One definition of self-improvement includes a willingness to address the needs of others and be generous with personal resources. When it comes to service and sacrifice, there is a marked difference in the choices of the churched and unchurched. One out of five unchurched people does not donate any time during a typical month to help people or organizations. Among those who do, the average amount of time donated is five hours per month. That's half as much time as most churched people, and the base of churched volunteers is considerably larger (only 3 percent fail to volunteer in a typical month).

Similarly, donating money is a struggle for the unchurched. Over the course of a year, churched people give away a median of $500 compared to $100 given by churchless people. The mean aggregate donation also shows a big disparity: $1,548 per year among the churched compared to $468 among the unchurched.

Reflections on Unchurched Lifestyles

When the unchurched observe the way most churched people live, they don't see much of a difference from themselves.

The distinctions revealed by the data in most areas are not large enough to cause much notice. (It may be worth noting that the areas where the churched and churchless differ the most—including consumption of sexually explicit media, volunteerism, and giving—are frequently choices made privately rather than public behaviors that might affect others' perceptions.) The similarities between the churched and the churchless offer to us a rebuke and an opportunity.

The rebuke is obvious and may be the first thing that comes to your mind: If churchgoers are no different in so many categories from the unchurched, our lives don't offer much incentive to become one of us. Jesus told his disciples, "If you belonged to the world, it would love you as its own" (John 15:19), and Paul challenged the church in Rome, "Do not conform to the pattern of this world, but be transformed by the renewing of your mind" (Romans 12:2). Christ's followers are called to be and live differently from the surrounding culture. With the help of the Holy Spirit, local faith communities must engage in some honest self-reflection to identify the ways we are conforming rather than being transformed.

Yet the similarities between the churched and the churchless also offer us an opportunity. When we think about how to connect with unchurched people, we may fare best when we offer them the same types of opportunities and experiences that appeal to us. In this sense, reaching the unchurched becomes an application of the Golden Rule: Do to the churchless what you would want them to do to you, if your roles were reversed.

Don't miss the fact that when the unchurched ponder how to become better human beings, a majority admit their best strategies revolve around God: obeying his rules, relying on his power and guidance, leaning into his grace, imitating the behaviors of Bible heroes, and so on. This is where churches can help. Churches are in a unique position to show people the way to Christ and all that he offers: new life, a new identity, a new set of values, restored relationships, new types of goals. As we'll see in more detail in chapter 14, there's no question that being a part of a church typically enriches people both spiritually and relationally. When the unchurched come looking for a better way of life, churches can show the way.

 Forward Thinking

- In what ways does your faith community stand out from the surrounding culture? In what ways do you blend in?
- How can your church follow the Golden Rule when it comes to connecting with unchurched people?
- How is your church equipping people to consume media wisely? How can you be a resource for both churched and unchurched people who want to think critically about their media consumption?

1 in 4 unchurched adults
are skeptics—either atheists
or agnostics

The Evolving Profile of the Skeptic

In the past two decades, some significant demographic shifts
have happened among American skeptics as a group.

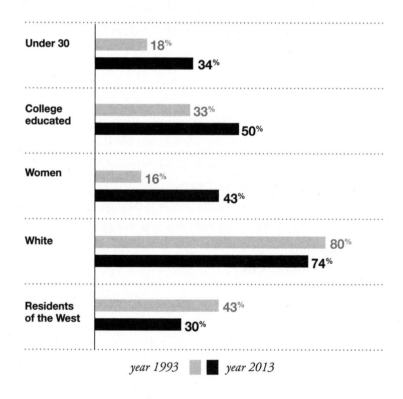

Under 30
18%
34%

College educated
33%
50%

Women
16%
43%

White
80%
74%

Residents of the West
43%
30%

year 1993 *year 2013*

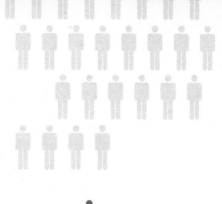

12

REACHING THE SKEPTICS

*Atheists and Agnostics Are a Different Brand
of Unchurched People*

As we noted in chapter 1, there are dozens of ways we might categorize those who do not attend church, depending on what demographic variables we prioritize or downplay (just as there are dozens of ways we could categorize church attenders). When we categorize people based purely on their set of beliefs, the skeptics emerge as a unique group among the churchless.

Skeptics are either atheists (they do not believe God exists) or agnostics (they are not sure God exists, but are open to the possibility). They have many different names in sociological and theological circles, but to those in the ministry trenches the skeptics are, crassly put, the top outreach prize. Effective ministry to skeptics results not only in church attendance but, more important, in their acceptance and embrace of Christ as Savior and Lord.

Skeptics represent a quarter of all unchurched adults (25 percent). Nearly one-third (31 percent) have never attended a Christian church service in their lives. That's almost double the proportion of the "virgin unchurched" among the churchless who are not skeptics (17 percent). Let's explore the ways skeptics differ from other unchurched adults.

Demographic Shifts among the Skeptics

The profile of a typical skeptic is different today from a decade or two ago. Today's skeptic, like her counterpart from two decades ago, is defined by her denial of or doubts about God's existence. But that is about the only thing she has in common with the unchurched atheist or agnostic of yesteryear.

Skeptics today are, on average, younger than in the past. Twenty years ago 18 percent of skeptics were under thirty. Today that proportion has nearly doubled to 34 percent. By the same token, the proportion of skeptics who are sixty-five or older has been cut in half, down to just 7 percent of the segment.

It is increasingly common among young adults to dismiss religion, God, churches, authority, and tradition. Many of them embrace the idea of being "spiritual but not religious." To some this means being in tune with their inner self without any kind of supernatural guidance or strength.

Their spirituality is self-contained, and their life perspective is, in general, self-centered. They are less interested in rules and regulations than other churchless people. They determine their own sense of right and wrong, values, meaning, and purpose. Their hope is in themselves, and most have little doubt that such hope is well placed. To Christians who acknowledge the essential fallenness of all humans (including themselves), this self-assurance may seem inappropriate or even absurd.

Today's skeptics tend to be better educated than in the past. Two decades ago, one-third of skeptics were college graduates, but today half of the group has a college degree. For years some observers have claimed that colleges and universities are a breeding ground for anti-God sentiment. While some on the secular Left have dismissed these claims as the paranoia of conservatives, the data afford some support for the notion that college campuses are comfortable places for young people to abandon God and assume total control of their own lives.

Perhaps the biggest transition of all is the entry of millions of women into the skeptic ranks. In 1993 only 16 percent of atheists and agnostics were women. By 2013 that figure had nearly tripled to 43 percent. This enormous increase is not because the number of skeptic men has declined; their numbers have steadily increased over the last two decades—but not nearly as rapidly as among women. It is interesting to note that, given the educational attainment of skeptics, the proportion of women who earned college degrees also rose substantially during roughly the same time frame.[15]

Religious skepticism has become more racially and ethnically inclusive. While whites represented 80 percent of all skeptics twenty years ago, that figure dropped to 74 percent by 2013. This is largely a reflection of the increased Hispanic and Asian populations among the skeptics. Asian Americans, the least-Christian ethnic demographic in the United States, tend especially to embrace skepticism. However, the recent sex scandals in the Catholic church have prompted a growing number of Hispanic people to surrender their faith in God along with their trust in religious leaders and institutions— though Hispanics, along with blacks, still remain less likely than other groups to accept the idea of a world without God. Whites, who constitute two-thirds of the total population, are well above average in their embrace of atheism and agnosticism; they comprise three-quarters of the skeptics.

In decades past, the Northeast and West were seen as isolated hotbeds of atheism and agnosticism. But that, too, has changed. While many leaders of the atheist movement are located in those areas, the skeptic population is now broadly dispersed across all regions. In fact, the Northeast has gone from being the second-most prolific region for skeptics to the least likely home of skeptics—even less than the Midwest and South. The West, which was home to 43 percent of skeptics in the early 1990s, is now home to just 30 percent of them. In our view, the reasons for this shift include population mobility, the standardizing impact of the media, the declining influence of churches and strong families in the Midwest and South, and the spread of skepticism among young, educated adults.

In many ways, skeptics now resemble the rest of America more than they once did. And their numbers are growing more quickly than anyone could have expected twenty years ago.

A Skeptic's Life

When asked about their primary goals, skeptics are much more likely to identify issues related to money (earning more, saving more, reducing expenses, budgeting better) and their physical condition (losing weight, eating better, getting healthier) compared to unchurched people who believe in God. They mention money goals five times more often and physical goals twice as often as other churchless people.

Skeptics are more likely to lean liberal: four out of ten (39 percent) describe themselves as liberal on social and political matters, double the proportion among the God-believing unchurched (21 percent) and more than triple the proportion among those who regularly attend a Christian church (11 percent). Relatively few skeptics describe themselves as conservative (9 percent) compared to other unchurched (26 percent) and regularly churched (52 percent) adults.

Skeptics rank much lower than any other group we studied not only on love of God but also on concern for the well-being of others. Yet they ranked highest on the various measures that relate to personal advancement and achievement. It is plausible that many consider a moral code that is others-centered as potentially blocking their quest for personal success.

Faith and Folly

Just as believers arrive at their belief in God by amassing a variety of information and experiences, skeptics piece together different inputs to draw their conclusion. It seems, however, that the three primary components that lead to disbelief in God's existence are (1) rejection of the Bible, (2) a lack of trust in the local church, and (3) the cultural reinforcement of a secular worldview.

Skeptics dismiss the idea that the Bible is holy or supernatural in any way. Two-thirds contend that it is simply a book of well-known stories and advice, written by humans and containing the same degree of authority and wisdom as any other self-help book. The remaining one-third are divided between those who believe the Bible is a historical document that contains the unique but not God-inspired accounts of events that happened in the past, and those who do not know what to make of the Bible but have decided it deserves no special treatment or consideration.

Even with those beliefs about the Bible, six out of ten skeptics still own at least one copy. Most have read from it in the past, and a handful (almost exclusively agnostics) still read it at least once a month. This is all to say that most skeptics have some firsthand experience with the Bible, and most had some regular exposure to it during their youth. For Christians who trust the notion that God's Word will not fail to produce fruit (see Isaiah 55:11), that early exposure encourages the hope that skeptics will someday reconsider their rejection of God. Until then, however, skeptics see the Bible as a book that may contain some good advice and even historical insights, but not a holy, powerful, and life-changing message from an omnipotent universal Being.

US churches have done little to convince skeptics they are wrong. In fact, because *more than two-thirds of skeptics have attended Christian churches in the past*—most for an extended period of time—their dismissal of God, the Bible, and churches is not theoretical in nature. Most skeptics think of Christian churches as:

- groups of people who share a common physical space and have some common religious views, but are not personally connected to each other in meaningful or life-changing ways

- organizations that add little, if any, value to their communities; their greatest value stems from the limited times they serve the needy in the community

- organizations that stand for the wrong things—wars, preventing gay marriage and a woman's freedom to control her body, sexual and physical violence perpetrated on people by religious authority figures, mixing religious beliefs with political policy and action

- led by people who have not earned their positions of influence by proving their love of humankind, and thus are not deserving of trust

Many of these ideas are initiated, promoted, and reinforced by celebrity personalities and media exposure. Sean Penn, the award-winning actor and film director, is a politically active citizen whose views about churches are often mixed into his comments on social problems. In an interview with *Rolling Stone* magazine that profiled his work helping victims of the devastating earthquake in Haiti, he remarked, "What it comes down to are the churches are not operating like instruments of love. They're hate machines. They're ignorance factories."[16]

Illusionist Penn Jillette is also an outspoken critic of religion in general and Christianity specifically. He expresses his feelings about matters of faith in his books, stage act, YouTube videos, and interviews. For example:

> I believe that there is no God. I'm beyond atheism.
> Atheism is not believing in God. Not believing in
> God is easy—you can't prove a negative, so there's
> no work to do.[17] . . . Religion cannot and should not
> be replaced by atheism. Religion needs to go away
> and not be replaced by anything. Atheism is not
> a religion. It's the absence of religion, and that's a
> wonderful thing.[18]

Another high-profile spokesman for atheism is Bill Maher, host of various programs and specials carried by HBO, the nation's leading pay channel. On his program *Real Time with Bill Maher*, he explained how he regards religion:

We are a nation that is unenlightened because of religion. I do believe that. I think that religion stops people from thinking. I think it justifies crazies. I think flying planes into a building was a faith-based initiative. I think religion is a neurological disorder. If you look at it logically, it's something that was drilled into your head when you were a small child. It certainly was drilled into mine at that age. And you really can't be responsible when you are a kid for what adults put into your head.[19]

These are just three examples of a new stratum of anti-religion celebrity apologist that also includes Sam Harris, Richard Dawkins, Stephen Hawking, Peter Singer, Woody Allen, Philip Roth, Julia Sweeney, and the late Christopher Hitchens. It's a chicken-or-egg conundrum to identify which came first: the atheist celebrity or the massive uptick in the number of atheists. Whatever the case, atheism has shifted in the past fifty years from cultural anathema to what all the cool kids are doing.

A Path to the Skeptic's Heart?

Is it foolish to believe Christians can help motivate skeptics to reconsider the truth about Jesus Christ? Absolutely not. The list of skeptics who have abandoned the godless world-view in favor of a life with Christ is long and inspiring—from academics C. S. Lewis and Alister McGrath to scientists Francis Collins and Rosalind Picard, to name a few. But it is imperative for Christians to remember that facilitating someone's transition from atheism to a God-centered, grace-filled life does not depend on our cleverness or persuasiveness. People come to Christ in many ways—and attendance at church events is certainly one of those—but it is God's Spirit who transforms a person's heart, mind, and soul. We may be used in that process, partnering with God in his holy work, but spiritual restoration is never accomplished through our abilities or talents.

With that limitation in mind, we can proceed with purposeful, intelligent, and realistic efforts to connect with skeptics. Our research offers some clues regarding the dos and don'ts of effectively impacting skeptics. For instance, by studying more than a dozen common outreach approaches, we identified what methods have the best chance of capturing their attention long enough for them to consider visiting a local church.

- Impersonal media efforts are almost guaranteed to be ignored. No skeptics we interviewed said they were "much more likely" to consider attending a church if they received a direct mail solicitation or had exposure to advertising about a nearby church via television, radio, newspapers, or billboards.

- Fewer than one out of ten skeptics said they might consider attending if a friend invited them to a church service; if they received a telemarketing call from someone they did not know; if they encountered the church through some type of social marketing or other online experience; or if they heard a sermon via a podcast, CD, or some other means. Discovering that a church had multiple locations in the area also did little to motivate them.

- Among the most hopeful means of connecting with skeptics were events open to the public, such as concerts or seminars, sponsored by a church (10 percent said this might make them much more interested in a church). Also showing promise were projects undertaken by a church designed to help the needy in the community, resulting in a reputation for loving the poor (mentioned by 12 percent).

- The approach rated highest by skeptics (14 percent) revolved around having a congregation in which the older people regularly connected with and shared life experiences with younger adults. Considering that a large share of skeptics are younger adults, many of whom have grown up without effective parenting or mentoring, the desire for this kind of practical, hands-on life assistance makes sense.

One of the unexpected results we uncovered is the limited influence of personal relationships on skeptics. Our long-term research shows that these individuals are considerably less relational and less engaged in social activities than the norm. Even the events they attend are less about meeting like-minded people than about having a desired experience

CHURCHLESS

Outreach Efforts Likely to Cause Skeptics to Be "Much More Likely" to Attend a Church

Outreach activity	Skeptics	Non-skeptic unchurched
Learned that the church has older adults who provide life lessons and advice to younger adults	14%	21%
The church undertakes a lot of activity to help the poor and needy in the community	12	25
Interesting events, such as concerts or seminars, that are open to the public sponsored/hosted by the church	10	23
Invited by a friend to attend their church, they would accompany you to the service	7	25
Heard a sermon by the pastor online, via CD, or through a podcast, and liked what you heard	6	13
The church taught people how to avoid the negative effects of media and technology	6	15
The people met in each others' homes, instead of a church building, for prayer, worship, teaching, and conversation	5	16
The church had a significant and appealing presence online/through social networks	5	8
The church had multiple locations nearby	3	11
Someone you did not know called you on the telephone to describe the church and invite you to attend it	2	13
The church's pastor visited your home to tell you about the ministry and to invite you to attend a service	0	21
Someone who attends the church visited your home, conducted a survey about faith and spirituality, then invited you to attend their church	0	13
You saw billboards advertising the church	0	10
You saw advertisements for the church on television, radio, or in newspapers	0	10
You received information about the church in an advertisement received in the mail	0	7

Source: Barna Group, OmniPoll, conducted February 2010

or gaining helpful information. This raises some red flags for the many churches whose battle cry is "ministry is about relationships." The skeptics are not as enamored of relational bonds as are those who invest themselves in church life.

Reflections on Connecting with Skeptics

The pastor of the Vineyard in Ventura, California, is Bob Harper. He suggests that skeptics, in particular, do not reject the gospel because of Christians' hypocrisy or lifestyle choices:

> A lot of Christians think that if only the unchurched could see "Jesus' love in action" (feeding the hungry, etc.) they would want the message. In my experience, however, unchurched people think the Bible and the gospel are cultural artifacts that are no longer relevant. The unchurched audience is rejecting the church for worldview issues. . . . The bottom line is, we evangelicals are answering questions no one is asking.

To help his faith community answer questions the unchurched *are* actually asking, Bob and the other leaders have begun to focus their outreach efforts on introducing the Vineyard folks to the "skeptic's perspective." He says, "The 'evangelical perspective' does not address the concerns of anyone other than evangelicals. [Sociologist and author] James Davison Hunter says that Christians need to stop talking for a while. This is probably true." Listening, instead of talking, may be the best way to connect with those who don't share Christian worldview assumptions. If we don't take time to hear where skeptics—or any churchless people, for that matter—are coming from and what they're saying, we're not really in a conversation . . . we're just waiting for our chance to preach.

Treating skeptics as if they have a spiritual void is likely to be perceived as offensive. Let's remember that rejecting belief in our God is not the same as being without faith. Most skeptics have an abundance of faith—in themselves. We must respect their self-reliance, rather than try to convince them of its ultimate folly. Remember, it is not our job to change hearts and minds; that duty falls exclusively under the Holy Spirit's job description. Rather, it is our job to be the presence of Christ to those around us. And as a close reading of the Gospels reveals, Jesus was as likely to ask questions as he was to offer answers. In our relationships with skeptics, let's do the same.

Forward Thinking

- What outreach methods is your church using in an effort to connect with skeptics? Given the research into the effectiveness of various methods, what could you do differently to have a greater impact?

- Have you and your faith community thought much about worldviews? How could you better understand the "skeptic's perspective"?

- In your conversations with skeptics, are you more likely to ask questions or offer answers? What could you do to be the presence of Christ in those relationships?

What works

▼

An invitation from a trusted friend

An in-home visit from a pastor or church member

An appealing event—such as a concert or seminar—hosted at the church

Ministries that regularly and effectively serve the poor

Mentoring and development opportunities for young adults

▲

Attracting the Churchless to Your Church

▼

Direct mailings from the church

TV, newspaper, billboard, or radio advertisements

Unsolicited phone calls

Relying on the church website

Celebrity guest speakers at the worship service

▲

What doesn't

Get full color infographics from this book at www.barna.org/churchless

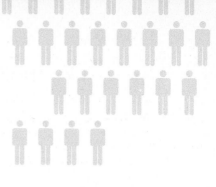

13

FAITH, FUTURE TENSE

*The Faith Experience and Spiritual Journey Unchurched
Adults Are Seeking*

Because most are optimistic by nature, many church leaders believe that if they work long and hard at appealing to the unchurched, they will eventually succeed at attracting them to church services. Is this approach likely to succeed? One value of research is that it can provide a realistic assessment of opportunities and obstacles.

Overall, just one out of seven (14 percent) unchurched adults in the United States appears open to trying a new church. Yet, projected across the aggregate unchurched universe, this percentage represents nearly 16 million people—not a sum of souls to dismiss! And the figure may actually be more promising than imagined: only two-fifths of these individuals are born-again unchurched folks, the likeliest segment to target. This means that three out of five people open to trying church are not born again. Women, singles, and nonpracticing Catholics also emerged as more interested in the possibility.

Attracting unchurched people to the flock, however, demands a variety of entry points. About half of the church-less said they would prefer that their route to the church world be through exposure to a church's worship service; the other half would prefer a different initial type of exposure.

Prime Touch Points

Churches have demonstrated tremendous creativity in seeking to attract churchless people to church. To estimate the current appeal of some of those strategies, we asked the unchurched to rate how much influence each of thirty approaches or components might have on their interest in attending a church. Keeping in mind that the quality of execution of a specific strategy is critical regardless of people's predisposition, their responses provide a better understanding of their mind-set.

The three approaches that generally seemed to have the most positive effect on the potential for returning to church were developing relationships, sponsoring events, and culti-vating a positive reputation and related awareness.

Relational Tactics

One out of every five unchurched adults would be much more interested in attending a specific church if a trusted friend personally invited them and agreed to attend alongside them. This approach has been the highest-rated tactic in the twenty-plus years that we have been tracking the unchurched and how to interest them in attending a church. Interestingly, the percentage of unchurched adults who expressed a positive reaction to this approach in our most recent study is the lowest we have registered during that time period. That is a reflection of how American culture is changing—and how important it is for churches to be informed about alterations in what does and does not work in reaching out to those who live completely outside the walls of the church community.

However, it is important to realize that while personal invitations from trusted friends put specific churches on the radar of unchurched individuals, they remain far from convinced that they should attend that church. According to a subsequent question about this progression, only 4 percent said they would "definitely" attend the church if accompanied by their friend, and the others would continue to do their homework about the church and determine how much they really wanted to enter the church world.

One other relational approach that drew a surprisingly strong positive response was receiving an in-home visit from the pastor or a church member to discuss the possibility of attending the church. One out of every six churchless adults said they would be much more interested in the church if they received such a visit.

Home visitation was the heartbeat of seeking unchurched people for many years. It fell out of style in the eighties and nineties as Americans became more protective of their time and space and actually took offense at such an intrusion. Now, however, in an increasingly depersonalized society there seems to be a somewhat greater openness to an in-home or other face-to-face conversation.

Event Marketing

One out of every five unchurched people indicated that they would be much more interested in considering a church if they attended an appealing event, such as a concert or seminar, that was sponsored by a nearby church. One of the challenges, of course, is to offer a high-quality event that intersects with the personal interests of a large enough number of unchurched individuals to justify the effort and the related costs. Unchurched people maintain high standards for such events; the competition is not other church events but all of the public offerings available in the entertainment and business worlds. Assuming that the event is professionally conducted, many churchless people see that adventure as a "safe" way of being introduced to the people, environment, and culture of the sponsoring church.

Reputational Appeal

Because the unchurched are skeptical about the value that churches have to offer, the reputation of the ministry plays an important role in attracting those who often feel burned, disappointed, or misunderstood by churches. The research shows that two of the most important ways to be positioned in the minds of the unchurched are first, as a ministry that regularly and effectively serves the needs of the poor, and second, as a church that understands young people and provides the kind of mentoring and development they need to thrive in life.

Notice that the unchurched show little interest in attending a church known for the quality of its worship music or even the quality of its sermons. Millions of churchless adults are very sensitive to the balance between teaching and street-level ministry; they fear getting connected to a congregation that is all talk and no action.

Moderate Potential

Two outreach alternatives held appeal for a significant, but not overwhelming, proportion of the unchurched. One of those was the possibility of participating in a house church rather than a conventional church ministry. This appealed to 15 percent of the churchless, but was of greatest interest to people under thirty, born agains, and blacks. Each of those subgroups showed twice as much interest in a house church as did other churchless segments.

Another possibility was inviting the unchurched to a gathering of people from the same age group and general lifestyle as the churchless adult, for a social time like a picnic or sports outing. This, too, appealed to about 15 percent of the unchurched. The catch is that such an event cannot be a veiled attempt to gather a captive audience for exposure to a church sales pitch. The objective of the unchurched is to get a sense of what the people are like. If the congregation passes the "test," a positive experience at the event might lead to a visit to the church. The unchurched are in no rush to find a church home, and they do not want to find themselves in an uncomfortable situation as they scout out the possibilities.

Losing Strategies and Tactics

The research confirms what so many churches have learned the hard way: most approaches not only fail to attract unchurched people, but might actually discourage them from considering other church options in the future. The following approaches are likely to fall flat, with less than 10 percent of the churchless reporting they might be attracted by such efforts:

- information about a church provided through the mail

- advertising for a church on TV, in a newspaper, or on the radio

- an unsolicited phone call from someone representing a church in the community to describe the church and offer an invitation to attend

- advertising for the church on a local billboard

- a website that describes the church and invites people to attend

- a sermon from the pastor on CD or podcast

- emphasizing that the church has multiple locations in the community

- providing entry to a "video church"—a ministry that has a real-time video feed of live teaching from the main location, with live music and leadership at the remote location

- a contemporary seeker service

- showing a Hollywood-quality movie at the church that deals with issues like marriage, faith, or parenting

- providing a book club that discusses books about faith and life

- offering an open-mic discussion group or online chat that focuses on questions related to faith and spirituality

- a celebrity guest speaker appearing at a church's worship services

Since this list of activities contains a range of efforts often employed by churches, let's take a minute to explore what this list does and doesn't mean. First, just because most unchurched adults say they are not interested in a church website, for example, does not mean that churches should forgo having an effective web presence. When a churchless person decides to find a local church to visit, checking out the website is a common activity, and a church's digital content is often its only opportunity to make a first impression. In some ways, websites and social media efforts have become the new "front door" through which the unchurched—especially

Mosaic unchurched adults—come to experience church. It is absolutely necessary to be effective in the digital space, though this effort alone will not spell outreach success.

Second, most of the ideas on the list above fall flat because they are not what the churchless expect to find in today's churches. They don't need to go to a church to see a movie, listen to a celebrity speaker, participate in a book club, and so on. Yes, Christian leaders need to prayerfully and carefully consider innovative new ways to reach the unchurched— and redouble our efforts around classic relational forms of outreach—but we also need to be mission-minded above all else. In the end, people need Jesus—not spiritually oriented alternatives to the same activities offered by the local community center.

Finally, we have learned through our years of research that while some efforts, such as direct mail, may seem like attractive ways to reach the unchurched, there is potential for collateral damage to the reputation of our churches. Mass advertising efforts tend to work with a small minority of adults, leaving the majority with deepening skepticism toward Christians and faith communities. The message of Jesus and the invitation to participate in a local community are turned into a mere marketing campaign. Are there times when marketing should be employed, particularly in relational ways, such as giving people in your church invitation cards for their churchless neighbors? Yes! But every method should be adopted with the knowledge that what's at stake is much more than what kind of numbers we attract each Sunday. We are stewards of the truest story about humanity and God. We must take care not to cheapen the gospel by relying on marketing prowess to attract attenders.

Short-Term Missions

One more possible approach is offering the unchurched an opportunity to join a group of people from the congregation on a short-term mission trip. Such an adventure might last anywhere from three days to two weeks. Because the unchurched seem to highly value demonstrations of service to the needy, as well as the chance to actively participate in such efforts, a mission trip seems as if it would reflect an interest and meet a need for some people whose life without church might not afford such an opportunity.

Our advice, though, is to enter this arena with caution. The research discovered that less than one out of every twenty churchless adults is willing to consider such an intensive exposure to the church through such a trip. Among those who have gone on a mission trip in the past—that constitutes only 6 percent of the unchurched—two-thirds of them said they would be open to another such trip in the future. But among those who have never been on a missions-driven journey, very few harbor the inclination to spend the time, money, and effort on the venture.

Reflections on Reaching Out

As in the marketing of any product or service, the challenging reality is that you can do everything "right" and still fail to appeal to the target audience. Thousands of churches across the country can testify to that heartbreak.

The unchurched admit that they are not much interested in seeking a church home—and that if they decide to do so, they are likely to explore a single church and then give up the hunt. Three-quarters of them contend that they are no longer willing to do a more extensive church search; if the one ministry they decide to examine meets their needs, they'll pursue a relationship with that ministry, but they are not likely to visit and study other churches if the initial effort bombs.

Should this stop you from reaching out? Of course not. But choose your methods wisely. Instead of sinking significant money into paid advertising, which few churchless people seem inclined to respond to, consider how your resources might be better spent equipping church members to meet tangible and relational needs in your community. If young people in your neighborhood are without mentors or healthy friendships with older adults, how can you leverage your resources so your congregation is ready and able to meet that need? In-home visits are of increasing appeal to churchless adults. Is there a ministry group within your church that is already trained in this area, or will such outreach require new initiative, leaders, and resources? If event marketing is the way to go for your community, what will you do to ensure your church's events are of the highest possible quality (so your efforts don't have the opposite effect than what you're hoping for)?

There are dozens, maybe hundreds, of possible ways to connect with the unchurched in your area. And what turns out to be most effective in your community probably won't be exactly the same as what works elsewhere. But that's okay—good, even. For the Lord has called you to a particular place inhabited by particular people who are seeking the meaning, satisfaction, and fulfillment only a life with God can provide. Your faith community is uniquely gifted to bring that good news. Figuring out how to do it well will require humility, courage, and a commitment to asking the right questions.

Forward Thinking

- How are your church's resources currently deployed when it comes to outreach? How effective are these efforts? To use business-speak, what kind of return on investment (ROI) are you reaping?

- Assistance to the poor and mentoring the young are the two ministry areas that most impress unchurched people as essential to the heart of a church. Do you agree that these ministry areas are central to the church's mission? Why or why not? How is your church doing in these areas?

- Relational appeal remains the most powerful incentive for churchless people to visit or connect with a church. How well or poorly are your members doing when it comes to inviting friends and family to church? What could make it easier or more natural for them to offer such invitations?

What value is the church?

godly relationships | doing good | peace

worship | wisdom | witness | mentoring

unity | discernment | faith focus

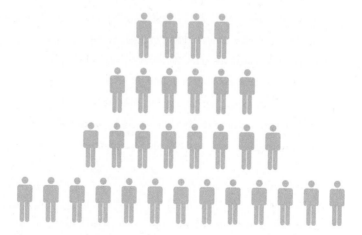

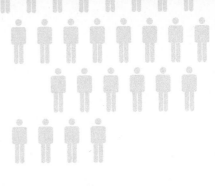

14

WHY CHURCHES MATTER

Advocating for Church in a Post-Christian Culture

Over the course of this book we've looked at the unchurched from a number of angles, considering their lifestyles, beliefs, values, and faith practices. We have considered how best to connect with the churchless and bring them into the fold. Yet in the end, we have to answer a key question: Why should people go to church?

A majority of Americans no longer believe Christianity is the default faith of the nation, and a rapidly expanding segment of the population is questioning the purpose and value of both churches and church engagement. Reacting to teaching that equates one's absence from Sunday morning services with sin, and to leaders who see in the loss of membership a sign of flagging commitment, many Americans are flaunting their individuality and self-determination. Millions of citizens are exercising their freedom of choice and disassociating from institutions and traditions of all kinds—not only religious assemblies. Formerly respected institutions such as marriage, banks, courts, unions, and schools are greeted with skepticism. It's a tough era for any organization that relies on people's trust to remain effective.

Painful as it may be to consider, the doubters raise legitimate questions that deserve thoughtful answers. In a society where personal choice and independence are among the most esteemed values, why would someone participate in communal church life? Why should anyone devote precious time, energy, money, and loyalty to a Christian church?

If we hope to stem the swelling tide of churchless adults, we must make a compelling case for the value of church life. If nothing else, having good reasons to participate in the congregational adventure can remind us why we stay committed to our faith community.

The Value of Church

Christian churches come in a dazzling array of sizes, locations, beliefs, organizational structures, and missions. With about 320,000 Protestant churches, more than 18,000 Catholic parishes, and more than 50,000 house churches open for business in the United States, church options abound. And while these worshiping communities are diverse, they hold several elements in common.

- *Godly relationships.* Churches provide a place to connect with others who experience similar challenges and seek similar life goals, a place where people know they belong. Forming relationships within a broader community gives people an opportunity to think and live consistently with a viable worldview and to be lovingly supported in pursuit of a common way of life.

- *Doing good.* Although Americans tend to be self-centered, most of us also have a desire to make a difference for good in the world. We can sometimes accomplish a positive impact through our personal, isolated efforts. Often, however, we leave our mark on the world by joining with people whose efforts multiply the effect of our own. Churches organize and facilitate abundant good works that affect the world in large and small ways, from individual to national impact, from local to international in scope. Our research suggests that the total value of volunteer hours contributed to US churches, plus the money donated for charitable and ministry activities, exceeds $200 billion annually. That's a lot of generosity in economic terms, but the value in human terms is incalculable.

- *Peace.* In a society where fast action and endless noise is the norm, many churches are a place where people can be still and silent in God's presence. Churches are one of the few places where a person can seek

emotional and spiritual sanctuary from the daunting
pressures of the day. While no church worth its
biblical salt condones escapism, neither does any
church with a heart turn its back on those who need a
safe place to think and reflect.

- *Worship.* As part of a church community, people can
unite with others in humble worship, recalibrating
their focus away from self-centeredness and
distraction. A regular time of corporate devotion to
God can be transformative.

- *Wisdom.* Information is ubiquitous but insight is
rare. Churches often provide genuine wisdom to
people through a variety of resources, forums, and
interactions. Those who engage with a church may
learn more about God, themselves, and the world—or
all of the above.

- *Witness.* Christians have a responsibility to share their
knowledge of and experience of Jesus Christ with
people who do not have a relationship with him. The
full burden of that commitment does not rest on the
shoulders of any one person, though; the congregation
exists as a body of fellow sojourners whose love for
one another witnesses to the Good News of Christ.
By being a place where spiritual seekers can encounter
a variety of Jesus' followers and a range of faith
experiences, the local church provides an introduction
to God and the Christian journey.

- *Mentoring.* Millions of parents bring their children to churches, sometimes even when they do not personally have much interest in Christianity. They do so for many reasons, but chief among them is to introduce their kids to other children and adults with good values and strong morals, in a safe and positive environment. Such environments, beyond the church, are less common by the day. Churches offer families a community of friends and mentors, as well as a chance to support, encourage, and mentor others.

- *Unity.* At their best, churches are places where people of different genders, generations, ethnic groups, and socioeconomics come together to love, serve, and learn from one another. In our highly fragmented society, this is a rare and beautiful glimpse of God's Kingdom breaking in to tear down divisions and unite his diverse people with one Spirit.

- *Discernment.* Churches, when they are engaged with their surrounding communities, are places of cultural discernment—a commodity in too-short supply. Various aspects of culture can either nourish or destroy but, in the thick of it, it's not always obvious which outcome is which. Faith communities are places where it's possible to take a step back and observe—with a Bible in one hand and a newspaper (or smartphone) in the other—our culture and its effects on human flourishing, rather than mindlessly consuming whatever content is blasted in one's general direction.

- *Faith focus.* Above all else, Christian churches are places where people can grow in their pursuit of Jesus. Faith, as they say, is like a muscle; it gets stronger only when it is exercised. Churches provide the coaches, exercise partners, and training facilities that help faith grow stronger. While the world offers an endless assortment of distractions, churches are designed to narrow our focus to the thing that truly matters: letting our lives reflect Jesus more and more every day.

This book would be incomplete if we did not also provide a data-driven argument for the importance of church engagement. After thirty-plus years of studying the relationship between beliefs and behaviors, we have identified a correlation between church engagement and a number of desirable life outcomes.

Comparing the life experiences of the unchurched with those of the actively churched reveals that churchgoers are less likely to be stressed out and to feel lonely. They are more likely to say they are happy, are making a positive difference in the world, have deep connections with their friends, and are fulfilling their calling in life. (See the next table.)

Barna Group is not the only research organization to identify these trends. In a massive study of more than 300,000 Americans' emotional well-being, in which at least 1,000 US adults were surveyed each day about the positive and negative emotions they experienced, Gallup discovered that regular churchgoers experience more positive and fewer negative emotions than those who do not regularly attend religious services.[20] These stats track with the overall findings of Gallup's research in this area, which confirms that religious Americans enjoy greater all-around well-being than those who are not religious.[21]

Church engagement is not a cure-all, but the data indicate that churchgoers are more likely to experience some of the life outcomes desired by churchless and churched alike.

The Actively Churched Are More Likely to Experience Positive Life Outcomes

Life outcome experienced	Actively churched	Unchurched
Am making a positive difference in the world[a]	86%	67%
Happy[b]	85	80
Have deep, soul connections with my friends[c]	82	69
Believe I am fulfilling my calling in life[d]	81	64
Stressed out[b]	32	37
Lonely[b]	15	22

Source: Barna Group, Ventura, CA; [a]OmniPoll 1-08, January 2008, 451 actively churched, 277 unchurched; [b]OmniPoll 1-13, January 2013, 460 actively churched, 582 unchurched; [c]OmniPoll 3-08, August 2008, 482 actively churched, 305 unchurched; [d]OmniPolls S-08/2-08, May–July 2008, 818 actively churched, 632 unchurched

The Deepest Value

The highest value of being part of a faith community is not the personal benefits we may receive. We can understand the value of church engagement more deeply, as well.

God created us for communion with him and with one another. The biblical account of creation invites us to glimpse his purposes in creating people in his image; in Eden, we see humans in perfect relationship with God and at peace with each other (see Genesis 1–2). According to Genesis 2:18, "It is not good for the man"—or anyone else!—"to be alone."

Through the unfolding time line of Scripture, we see God in relationship with *a people*—a group of people called together for his purpose. In most of the New Testament letters, written to the earliest generations of Jesus-followers struggling to understand their calling as God's people, the "you" to whom Paul, James, and Peter write is not singular; it is plural.

For better or worse—and seasons of both exist even in the best churches—Christians are called into community to be God's people. Jesus said the Greatest Commandment is actually *two* commandments: to love God and to love others (see Matthew 22:36-40; Luke 10:27; Mark 12:30-31). It's not obedience if we agree only to Part A.

Our highest calling is love for God and for others. Participating in the life of a local church—in whatever form—requires us to practice the fine art of loving. Church enables us to regularly and creatively express our love to God in worship. And it gives us endless opportunities to love others, warts and all, and to be loved by others . . . warts and all.

This is the deepest value of church.

Two Hurdles to Church Engagement

Some churchless people already recognize the value of church but can't clear the two main hurdles between them and deep engagement: (1) the sense that God is missing from church, and (2) the suspicion that Christians are missing the point.

Who Are We Here For?

Churches should be places where we experience God's presence in the company of his people. Sadly, however, a surprisingly large number of unchurched people tell us that, despite all the stellar programming they've experienced in church, the one thing they are seeking is a powerful, undeniable encounter with the living God—and they haven't found it yet. Of course, a person's spiritual readiness and attunement to God's Spirit are part of what makes him or her able to sense his presence. But many people who overcome the internal and external obstacles to visiting a church service do so exactly because they are spiritually ready and seeking to tune in to the Spirit. Sadly, some leave disappointed.

Despite all the opinions churchless (and churched) people offer about musical styles, architecture, sound systems, creativity, intellectualism, and the menu of programs provided by churches, none of these is the main attraction. These elements are nice sideshows, but people don't come to church for the carnival rides. They come to meet God. People complain about the uncomfortable seats and stale popcorn when center stage is empty of the main event.

Most Americans have plenty of other opportunities to

gather with people they don't know for conversation, music, education, and personal enrichment. But a local body of believers is the only place they can meet God together with his people. What a privilege to facilitate encounters with God week after week! When it's humble and sincere, it never gets old.

God never tires of being present with his people, so why would we settle for anything less than his presence? Yet it seems many churches do just that. Even churched people tell us they wonder where God is in their church experience. Our studies consistently show a large majority of people leave their church's service without feeling as though they have connected with God. If those who regularly attend depart with such disappointment and confusion, what must it be like for those who are new to the church adventure?

Every church is different, but here are some common elements that leave people feeling empty:

- The music portion of corporate worship feels like more of a performance or routine than a heartfelt offering to or proclamation of God.

- The teaching is designed to inform people about God rather than to usher them into his presence and enable a comprehensible connection with him.

- Public prayers seem more like scripted statements than authentic conversation with God, more like an extension of the teaching time, directed to the congregation rather than to the Lord.

- The offering is part of a routine in which people perform their duty rather than eagerly and thankfully returning a portion of the funds God has entrusted to them.

- There seems to be no compelling, consistent sense of reverence, awe, gratitude, expectancy, or honor associated with the worship activities. Instead, the rituals feel like comfortable habits performed without any expectation of God's presence or ability to guide the proceedings according to his purpose.

- Few congregants consider the event to be special; it seems, instead, a requirement they meet to placate God and protect their own interests.

- People come to the "worship show" without really connecting in a meaningful way with other believers; the service is essentially just a well-oiled "experience" machine that tries to impress people every week.

One of the simplest ways we can gauge our success at offering a true God-present experience is to ask one question: Do *we* encounter God? Do we plan the music, teaching, social hour, and everything else with the goal of connecting with him and his people? Or do those peripherals somehow take on a life of their own, crowding out the very Person they are meant to honor? If we can't honestly say that we, in community with God's people, meet with him at the services or

CHURCHLESS

events we plan, then we need to reexamine what is getting our attention. If God isn't, we're doing it wrong.

Who Are We Becoming?

As we described in previous chapters, the reputation of Christ's followers is not always spotless. More than four out of five non-Christian young adults (84 percent) say they personally know a Christian; but just 15 percent say that the lifestyles of the Christians they know are noticeably more positive than the norm.[22] When it comes to attracting people who wonder what difference faith in Christ might make in their lives, this disparity between faith and actions does Christians no favors. It lends credence to the notion that, whatever important things we claim to be doing in church, all our busyness and self-important activity amount to an adventure in missing the point.

In a recent study conducted in partnership with John Burke, author of *Mud and the Masterpiece*, Barna Group looked at whether Christians in America more closely resemble Jesus or the Pharisees.[23] Based on Scripture, we identified twenty specific actions and attitudes that might characterize a person as either Christlike or pharisaical, and asked Christians to respond with their preferences. For example, Christlike attitudes included, *I see God-given value in every person, regardless of their past or present condition* and *I feel compassion for people who are not following God and doing immoral things.* Pharisaical attitudes included, *I believe we should stand against those who are opposed to Christian values* and *People who follow God's rules are better than those who do not.* Taking our cues from the words and actions of Jesus, Christlike attitudes and actions were focused on loving others, while pharisaical attitudes and actions were more often focused on following rules.

The unfortunate reality is that most people who attend Christian churches land on the pharisaical end of the continuum. In fact, as the following pie chart shows, 51 percent of self-identified Christians are primarily pharisaical in both attitude and action; 14 percent are mostly pharisaical in attitude but more Christlike in behavior; and 21 percent are more Christlike in attitude but mostly pharisaical in their actions. The remaining one out of every seven (14 percent) tends to be more Christlike in both attitude and action.[24]

Are Self-Described Christians More Like Jesus or the Pharisees?

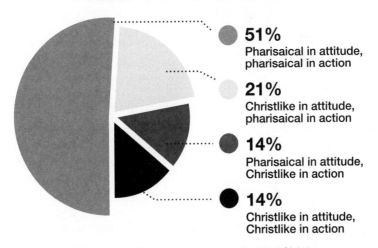

51%
Pharisaical in attitude, pharisaical in action

21%
Christlike in attitude, pharisaical in action

14%
Pharisaical in attitude, Christlike in action

14%
Christlike in attitude, Christlike in action

Source: Barna Group and John Burke, 2013; N=718 self-described Christians

Evangelical Christians, a small subset of the Christian population and the segment that is typically most immersed in church life, in bringing faith into the marketplace and in studying the Bible, emerged as the subgroup most likely to be Christlike. Yet even among evangelicals, less than one-quarter were classified as predominantly Christlike. Evangelicals, it turns out, tend to be more Christlike in activity than in attitude. In other words, they may well do the right things, but they often do them for the wrong reasons.

The other population segments we studied fared even worse. Among the people groups who struggle most with such spiritual confusion—some would eagerly call it hypocrisy—are people in their mid-sixties and older, Hispanics, and men.[25]

Does all of this remind you of Jesus' command to clean up our own act before we criticize others, to remove the two-by-four blocking our own vision before checking others' eyes for specks of dust? (See Matthew 7:1-5.) As the Coldplay lyric asks, "Am I a part of the cure? Or am I part of the disease?"[26] Imagine the impact more Christlike attitudes and actions—focusing more on loving others than on behavioral rules—would have on our attempts to draw the unchurched into relationship with Christ and healthy connection with a church community.

Strategy without Manipulation

We must not lose sight of the fact that appealing to the unchurched is a spiritual quest, not a business transaction or bottom-line proposition. But it is also important to be strategic in thought and action when it comes to how we share our faith with others. We have limited resources—time, money, relationships, opportunities—and an eternal purpose. How can we maximize our resources in cooperation with God to transform lives?

One strategic consideration is identifying how the Good News of Christ intersects with different people's priorities and phases of life. This is not to say that the gospel changes, but that different aspects of the Good News *sound like* good news to different people. For instance, a public defender or prisoner advocate might be very concerned about a corrupt justice system. A significant aspect of the gospel is that God is just, and his justice breaks into our world wherever Christ's followers live under his reign. To anyone who is seeking justice, that's good news.

Thirty years ago the most effective form of evangelism was widely believed to be a straight-out, in-your-face, confront-the-sinner declaration of salvation available through Christ. A decade or two ago, evangelism shifted to a focus on personal relationships, cultivated with eternity in mind. We believe we're undergoing another shift today, wherein doing good in the world is a powerful apologetic to those who are seeking God. Evangelism can happen in the marketplace, where Christian leaders run businesses with a biblical view of people, not taking advantage of them but aspiring to help them flourish. Evangelism can happen in the social sector, where we can show how much Jesus cares about "the least of these."

The churchless want to know what churched people are for, not just what we are against. Saying we are "for the cause of Christ" may make perfect sense to church insiders, but to unchurched ears it is vague at best and aggressive at worst. Could we be both more specific and more winsome? Let's find ways to describe the Good News in terms others can relate to—just as Jesus did in his preaching ministry.

Beyond figuring out how to communicate the heart of the gospel in fresh and relevant ways in an increasingly post-Christian culture, we should also consider how best to communicate with particular churchless people. "The unchurched" is a convenient way to think and talk about the population segment that is unconnected to a faith community—but that segment is made up of unique individuals with their own stories. The best outreach strategies in the world will fail if we are unable to see each churchless person we encounter as a singular, infinitely valuable bearer of God's image.

Whom should you pursue? That question can be answered only after your church has done the hard work of getting to know who the unchurched are in your community. Your approach will vary depending on whether you have a substantial born-again churchless segment in your neighborhood or more people who are purely unchurched—that is, those with no background of church involvement. Your goal in both cases is to connect with the unchurched around you, but the way you approach them will differ.

Loving the Churchless

In every case, our strategic decisions and tactical initiatives must be motivated by love.

Most churchless people aren't looking for a church. They're seeking an encounter with God. And even if they're not seeking him directly, the vast majority are seeking to experience the essence of who he is: love. According to the apostle John, God is love (1 John 4:8)—and, what's more, those who follow Christ should be known by their love (see John 13:35). In our experience, as believers practice loving attitudes and behavior toward others inside and outside their faith community, unchurched friends and family don't have to be talked into church participation. They seek it out, drawn by the promise of love.

Here at the end of our in-depth look at the unchurched in the United States, we offer five ways you can reflect Jesus' love to the churchless. We're not providing a formula for taking action. Rather, these are our humble suggestions for taking the head knowledge offered in this book and turning it into loving action toward unchurched people.

Sharing Jesus

A majority of born-again Christians (54 percent) say they have shared their faith in Christ with a non-Christian in the last year. But if so many millions of Christians are having evangelistic conversations, why does there seem to be so little impact? It may be we've become more complacent than we realize about proclaiming the Good News because there are

so many other ways people are exposed to gospel-related content in our media-saturated culture: books, radio, television,
billboards, events, Facebook posts that urge you to "Like" if
you love Jesus, and on and on. Have we outsourced the role
of being Jesus' spokespeople? In our effort to match culture's
progress note for note, is it possible we've lost something of
the original tune?

Maybe we've lost our urgency because we forget to see
people as individuals whom God loves. He loves us so much
he became one of us.

The data contain some good news. Our recent research
shows that Mosaic born-again Christians are more involved
in sharing their faith with non-Christians than believers in
older generations.[27] As a generation, Mosaics are more lost—
that is, they are less likely to be born again than are older generations (even when preceding generations were young adults
as Mosaics are now). But there is a countertrend of young
Christians for whom sharing the truth of Jesus has become
a necessity in the face of generational apathy. This impulse
toward evangelism does not define a majority of Mosaics, but
there are a sufficient number of them to make a profound
difference. In a dark cultural sea of moral and spiritual uncer-
tainty, their conviction is a steady light.

As the younger generation shows us, the first step to reen-
gaging the unchurched is reigniting our hearts for the lost.

Selfless Serving

Instead of serving, we want to be served. This is the basic
orientation of our sin nature.

Seeking the unchurched can sometimes serve ourselves rather than the churchless—it all depends on our motivation. Serving the unchurched is either humble obedience to the Great Commandment and the Great Commission, or irrefutable proof that we're super-spiritual Jesus-followers who can expect dozens of jewels in our heavenly crowns.

Pride makes a mockery of loving words and actions.

In our conversations with churchless people about Jesus or the Bible, for example, it might be tempting to focus on the elegance of our arguments rather than on the heart of the hearer. This is self-serving, not serving. Colossians 4:5-6 reminds us to let our conversations with outsiders be gracious and effective so that we might have the right word for everyone.

Does your kindness have strings attached? Are you hoping your churchless neighbor, coworker, or friend will come to church so your churched friends will be impressed? It comes down to whether you are more concerned with your reputation or Jesus' reputation. The Lord tells us that the pure in heart are blessed, for they shall see God (Matthew 5:8). Is your heart pure in your relationships with the unchurched?

"If I give all I possess to the poor and give over my body to hardship *that I may boast*, but do not have love, I gain nothing" (1 Corinthians 13:3, emphasis added). We must check and recheck our motives for reaching out to the churchless. Our efforts to serve them must be driven by love . . . and nothing else.

This means, for instance, that we have to be okay with the fact that some people—probably most unchurched people,

CHURCHLESS

in fact—will not respond in the way we hope. We must have the "longsuffering" that comes with loving others, trusting God to grow the seeds we plant (see Mark 4:1-20).

This is the paradox: an *agendaless* agenda. Of course we hope to see the unchurched committed to God and his people, but we can't control the outcomes of our efforts. Paul wrote that he "planted the seed, Apollos watered it, but God has been making it grow" (1 Corinthians 3:6). When Paul planted the seed of the gospel among the Corinthians, he could not see what God would eventually make of it.

In the first chapter of this book, we quoted German pastor Dietrich Bonhoeffer, who said, "The church is the church only when it exists for others." What we didn't point out in that opening chapter is the context of Bonhoeffer's remark: the imperative for the German church to stand up for Jews being persecuted and murdered by the Nazis. Of course there was a chance that some Jews might become Christ-followers because of German Christians' commitment to stand with them against a genocidal government. But that wasn't why Bonhoeffer joined the resistance, risking (and losing) his life. He did it because he knew God's people are called to serve others, without regard for ourselves—or for whether the people we serve respond in the way we hope.

How can you and your faith community serve the unchurched, motivated by nothing but love? The goal is to serve the churchless, not because it proves our spiritual self-worth, but because it's the Jesus thing to do.

Suffering With

In his book *Maximum Faith*, George offers this diagnosis of
most churchgoers:

> We read about the promises of God, but don't
> experience their fulfillment. We participate in the
> institutionalized church, but find it less meaningful
> and satisfying than expected. We read the Bible, but
> generally lack a true understanding of the text, miss
> its richness, and misinterpret its counsel. We vacillate
> between the letter and the spirit of the Law, and
> receive the hope of neither. We take solace in being
> religious but overlook the value of true spirituality.[28]

Could it be that the life of faith we offer to the churchless
is *too small*? George goes on to show, through data, interviews, and biblical wisdom, that suffering and brokenness
are necessary catalysts of spiritual transformation—but sadly,
many of our churches are too safe, too *nice*, to make the
most of struggle. At the very moment we are ready to genuinely grow—when our spiritual equilibrium is upset—a lot
of churches try to reset our equilibrium back to "normal."
In other words, George argues, churches' best intentions too
often subvert people's rare opportunities for real progress on
their spiritual journey.

What does this mean for the churchless? When we remember the majority of the unchurched are actually *de*-churched,
we must admit the possibility that our churches are somehow

enabling many people to stall out on their journey toward deep, transformative faith. If this is true, loving the church-less means confessing where we have failed to be communities that foster honesty and vulnerability. We must confess that we are sometimes complicit in the stalled spiritual journeys of the unchurched, and commit to becoming more effective as communities of transformation. We must ask ourselves if our church is a place that allows broken people to heal fully and then reorient their momentum toward God, without sliding back into spiritual inertia. Consider how we can become a church that doesn't avert our eyes from grief, disappointment, or doubt. Loving the churchless means *suffering with* them—which is the original meaning of the word *compassion*—and trusting God to use seasons of darkness to bring new life.

Discerning Culture

The fourth way we can love the churchless is by being effective interpreters of culture. A spiritual way to say this is *discernment*.

The Bible tells us that some things never change. For example, God does not change (Psalm 55:19). Jesus is the same yesterday, today, and forever (Hebrews 13:8). There is nothing new under the sun (Ecclesiastes 1:9). Yet we have too often encountered Christians who rely on these "true truths" so strongly they refuse to account for other truths that are a part of our reality.

God "changes times and seasons; he deposes kings and raises up others. He gives wisdom to the wise and knowledge to the discerning" (Daniel 2:21). Our God is also a God of change, and he wants us to be wise about what's happening here and now.

The prophet Daniel was a tremendous student of Babylonian science, art, and law who used his cultural discernment to incredible effect, eventually becoming, essentially, the secretary of state of the pagan society that had taken God's people into captivity. Or look at 1 Chronicles 12:32, where the tribe of Issachar is described as people who "understood the times" and who "knew what Israel should do."

What does discernment look like for us? We can bring to people a godly interpretation of "the times." For example, in our current research on the Bible we find that many people—especially Mosaics—want to know how the Bible applies to issues they face, such as parenting, finances, family conflict, sexuality, dating and relationships, and technology.[29] It's true that following Jesus isn't about gaining life improvement skills. But many people, throughout the ages, have desperately turned to Jesus for help with a present, felt need in their lives—only to discover the help he offers is beyond what they could have imagined.

When the churchless turn to our community of faith for help in their everyday lives, do they find wisdom? Do we offer a biblical worldview of the world we actually live in?

Praying for Hope

Finally, prayer is a powerful way to love the unchurched. Pray for your heart to be open and responsive. Pray for your church to become soil where people can grow. Pray for the unchurched who live on your street and work in your building and shop in your corner store and coach your kid's soccer team.

For three decades Barna Group has studied the impact and characteristics of effective churches. One of the most consistent patterns we have observed is a commitment to prayer—by the senior pastor, the leadership team and staff, the lay leaders, and, of course, the people in the pews. When we compare thriving churches with those that are struggling, we see that a top-to-bottom commitment to prayer so often makes the difference.

Prayer is the thread that weaves together the other four approaches to the churchless. Regular communion through prayer connects us to Jesus' heart for those who are far from him. It strips our motives for service of selfishness and ego. It ignites compassion and sustains through suffering, transforming us by God's presence with us. And it invites the Spirit to give us a God-sized view of our cultural reality.

It is our prayer that this book is knowledge that you and your church, led by the Spirit, will turn into wisdom for your mission.

> I pray for you constantly, asking God, the glorious
> Father of our Lord Jesus Christ, to give you
> spiritual wisdom and insight so that you might
> grow in your knowledge of God. I pray that your
> hearts will be flooded with light so that you can
> understand the confident hope he has given to
> those he called—his holy people who are his rich
> and glorious inheritance. I also pray that you will

understand the incredible greatness of God's power for us who believe him. This is the same mighty power that raised Christ from the dead. (Ephesians 1:16-20, NLT)

Appendix 1

About the Research

The contents of this book are based on extensive, ongoing, nationwide research conducted by Barna Group. We used data from twenty surveys, encompassing interviews with more than 20,000 churched and unchurched adults. The number of unchurched adults involved was 6,276.

These surveys were done using random digit-dial telephone samples for landlines and listed cell phone samples for calls to mobile phones. Each of the studies entailed completing interviews with a minimum of 1,000 randomly chosen adults. The samples were developed to provide a reliable representation of the national population of people ages eighteen or older living within the forty-eight continental states. The estimated maximum sampling error for each survey of 1,000 adults was plus or minus 3.1 percentage points at the 95 percent confidence level; the maximum sampling error estimate diminished as sample size increased. The number of interviews completed with cell-phone owners was based on federal government estimates of the number of cell-only households.

The January 2011, 2012, 2013, and 2014 surveys also included samples of approximately 1,000 adults conducted online. Those studies relied on a research panel called KnowledgePanel®, part of GFK Custom Research North America. It is a probability-based online non-volunteer access panel. Panel members are recruited using a statistically valid sampling method with a published sample frame of residential addresses that covers approximately 97 percent of US households. Sampled non-Internet households, when recruited, are provided a netbook computer and free Internet service so they may also participate as online panel members. KnowledgePanel consists of about 50,000 adult members (ages eighteen and older) and includes persons living in cell-only households.

In all of these surveys, regional and ethnic quotas were designed to ensure that the final group of adults interviewed reflected the distribution of adults nationwide and adequately represented the three primary ethnic groups within the United States (those groups that comprise at least 10 percent of the population: white, black, and Hispanic). Those quotas were based on current US Census Bureau data regarding the population. Additional quotas were employed to balance the gender of respondents included in the samples. Upon completion of a survey, the data were run and the demographic outcomes were compared to the census statistics on key demographic attributes. In some cases the full survey database was then statistically weighted to bring the database into closer approximation of the true population proportions.

Surveys Included in the Unchurched Database

Study conducted in:	Total sample	Unchurched adult sample
January 2008	1,004	277
May 2008	1,003	331
July 2008	1,005	301
August 2008	1,005	305
October 2008	1,014	327
November 2008	1,198	299
July 2009	1,003	315
September 2009	1,004	284
January 2010	1,008	240
February 2010	1,005	305
August 2010	1,002	368
December 2010	1,022	311
January 2011	1,622	615
August 2011	1,007	324
January 2012	2,025	920
March 2012	1,020	386
April 2012	1,062	340
May 2012	1,009	371
November 2012	1,008	338
January 2013	2,083	952
January 2014	1,024	556

Appendix 2

About Barna Group

Barna Group, which includes its research division, Barna Research Group, is a private, nonpartisan, for-profit organization under the umbrella of the Issachar Companies. Located in Ventura, California, Barna Group has been conducting and analyzing primary research to understand cultural trends related to values, beliefs, attitudes, and behaviors since 1984, when it was founded in Los Angeles by George Barna.

As a marketing research firm, it initially served a blend of Christian ministries, nonprofit organizations, and various media and financial corporations. The client roster has grown to include the military, government agencies, and many other businesses. However, it has remained a leader in the execution of faith-focused research, pioneering methodologies and language in that field, as well as providing many ground-breaking studies in a wide range of areas related to faith and ministry. During its three decades of work, Barna Group has carefully and strategically tracked the role of faith in America, developing one of the nation's most comprehensive databases on spiritual indicators. In 2009 David Kinnaman acquired majority ownership of Barna Group under the auspices of Issachar Companies, Inc., and serves as its president.

The company operates as a visionary research and resource company from its location in central California. The company's vision is to provide people with credible knowledge and clear thinking, enabling them to navigate a complex and changing culture. To fulfill that vision, Barna Group offers a range of customized research, resources, and training to serve churches, nonprofits, businesses, and leaders.

Barna Group provides primary research, diagnostic tools, print and digital resources, leadership development, training and keynote talks, and organizational enhancement. The company has worked with thousands of nonprofit organizations and churches across the country, including many Protestant and Catholic congregations, denominations, and faith leaders. Some of its notable clients have included the Salvation Army, World Vision, Compassion International, the American Bible Society, and Habitat for Humanity. It has also served mainstream business and nonprofit leaders at organizations such as Paramount, SONY, Walden Media, Easter Seals, CARE, the ONE Campaign, the Humane Society, the Bill & Melinda Gates Foundation, and NBC Universal. Media, churches, and educational institutions rely on Barna Group's work for insight into matters of faith and contemporary society. Barna Group's public opinion research is frequently quoted in major media outlets such as *USA Today*, the *Wall Street Journal*, Fox News, *Chicago Tribune*, the *New York Times*, the *Dallas Morning News*, and the *Los Angeles Times*.

For more information about Barna Group, please visit www.barna.org.

Appendix 3

Glossary of Terms

Generations

Mosaics (also called Millennials) are the generation born between 1984 and 2002.

Busters (sometimes called Gen-Xers) were born between 1965 and 1983.

Boomers were born between 1946 and 1964.

Elders were born in 1945 or earlier.

Patterns of Church Involvement

Nomads were once active in church and still consider themselves Christian, but are not currently connected to a faith community.

Prodigals are no longer active in church and no longer consider themselves Christian.

Exiles take faith seriously, but feel caught between church and culture.

Faithfuls are serious about faith and actively involved in a faith community.

Acknowledgments

Every book is the product of assistance from numerous people. To those who participated in this project—including the more than 20,000 people who freely gave us their time and ideas as part of the interviewing process, and the faithful leaders who shared their ministry experiences—we thank you for your generosity and guidance. We hope this book reflects your insights in a manner worthy of your contribution.

Barna Group operates as a team devoted to fulfilling an important mission. This project could not have been birthed, nurtured, and completed without significant contributions from each team member. Those stalwarts include Pam Jacob, Traci Hochmuth, Clint Jenkin, Robert Jewe, Elaina Buffon, Aly Hawkins, Bill Denzel, Irene Castillo, Elaine Klautzsch, Brad Abare, Jill Kinnaman, and Roxanne Stone. Special thanks to Aly Hawkins for her editing and writing assistance on this project.

Thanks also to the great people at Tyndale House Publishers, including Doug Knox, Jan Long Harris, Karin Buursma, and Sarah Atkinson.

We both wish to acknowledge the love and support of our families. We are grateful for the patience, sacrifice, and encouragement we receive from our wives and children.

Endnotes

1. Those resources include "Never On a Sunday," George Barna, Ventura, CA, Barna Research Group, 1990; "Re-Churching the Unchurched," George Barna, Ventura, CA, Issachar Resources, 2000; and *Grow Your Church from the Outside In*, George Barna, Ventura, CA: Regal Books, 2002.

2. When describing the current size of the unchurched population or its subgroups, or the demographic qualities of those populations, we have drawn from the surveys conducted in 2014 in order to provide the most current statistics.

3. The fifteen criteria used are: 1. do not believe in God; 2. identify as atheist or agnostic; 3. disagree that faith is important in their lives; 4. have not prayed to God (in the last week); 5. have never made a commitment to Jesus; 6. disagree the Bible is accurate in the principles it teaches; 7. have not donated money to a church (in the last year); 8. have not attended a Christian church (in the last year); 9. agree that Jesus committed sins; 10. do not feel a responsibility to "share their faith"; 11. have not read from the Bible (in the last week); 12. have not volunteered at a church (in the last week); 13. have not attended Sunday school (in the last week); 14. have not attended religious small group (in the last week); 15. do not participate in a house church (in the last year). The classifications were: post-Christian was classified as meeting at least 60 percent of the fifteen factors (i.e., nine or more factors satisfied); highly post-Christian required meeting at least 80 percent of the fifteen factors (i.e., twelve or more factors satisfied). For additional information about the study, go to https://www.barna.org/barna -update/culture/608-hpca.

4. For more information on TED Talks, see www.TED.com.

5. Sherry Turkle, *Alone Together: Why We Expect More from Technology and Less from Each Other* (New York: Basic Books, 2012).

6. See http://hispanics.barna.org/products/.

7. This majority is a combination of those who say they "strongly agree" and those who "somewhat agree" with the statement.

8. The "average" referred to in this paragraph is the mean.

9. The theological statements to which people respond in order to be classified as an evangelical include the following: believe that God is the all-knowing, all-powerful, perfect creator of the universe who still rules the world today; strongly agree that their religious faith is very important in their life today; strongly agree that the Bible is totally accurate in all of the principles it teaches; strongly agree that they have a personal responsibility to share their faith in Christ with people who believe differently; strongly disagree that when Jesus was on earth he sinned, like other people; strongly disagree that if people are good enough, or do enough good things for other people, they can earn their way into heaven; and strongly disagree that the devil, or Satan, is not a living entity but is just a symbol of evil. For more information about this classification approach, and the research that led to and supports it, visit https://www.barna.org/component/content/article/47-misc/647-definitions#.U1cAWeZdV9c.

10. See 2 Timothy 3:16.

11. David Kinnaman, *You Lost Me: Why Young Christians Are Leaving the Church . . . and Rethinking Faith* (Grand Rapids, MI: Baker, 2011).

12. In demographic literature a "traditional family" in the American context is generally defined as a married man and woman with two or more children under the age of eighteen.

13. For more information, see http://whatisorange.org/.

14. For more information regarding the impact of faith at an early age, see George Barna's books *Transforming Children into Spiritual Champions* (Ventura, CA: Regal Books, 2012) and *Revolutionary Parenting* (Carol Stream, IL: Tyndale House Publishers, 2007).

15. Women earned 54 percent of all college degrees in 1993; by 2010, women earned more than 60 percent of degrees.

16. Mark Binelli, "The Rolling Stone Interview: Sean Penn," *Rolling Stone* (February 19, 2009): 49.

17. Penn Jillette, "There Is No God," NPR series (November 22, 2005): http://www.npr.org/2005/11/21/5015557/there-is-no-god.

18. Penn Jillette, "Don't Replace Religion; End it," *New York Times* (January 22, 2013): http://www.nytimes.com/roomfordebate/2013/01/22/is-atheism-a-religion/atheism-should-end-religion-not-replace-it.

19. Quoted in *Pastors' Weekly Briefing*, February 25, 2005; 1.

20. Gallup-Healthways Well-Being Index, 2011. See http://www.gallup.com/poll/153374/Churchgoers-Boast-Better-Mood-Especially-Sundays.aspx.

21. Gallup-Healthways Well-Being Index, 2011. See http://www.gallup.com /poll/152723/Religious-Americans-Enjoy-Higher-Wellbeing.aspx.
22. Among the resources to examine are *unChristian*, David Kinnaman and Gabe Lyons (Grand Rapids, MI: Baker Books, 2008); *You Lost Me*, David Kinnaman (Grand Rapids, MI: Baker Books, 2011); *Maximum Faith*, George Barna (Strategenius Group: New York, 2011); and *The Seven Faith Tribes*, George Barna (Carol Stream, IL: Tyndale House Publishers, 2010).
23. For the most recent research on this matter, including the questions used in the survey, see, "Christians: More Like Jesus or More Like the Pharisees?" posted April 30, 2013, accessible at http://www.barna.org /faith-spirituality/619-are-christians-more-like-jesus-or-more-like-the -pharisees. Barna Group appreciates John Burke's permission to use this information for this book.
24. Ibid.
25. Ibid. Also see *Mud and the Masterpiece*, John Burke (Grand Rapids, MI: Baker Books, 2013).
26. From "Clocks," written by Guy Barryman, Jonathan Buckland, William Champion, and Chris Martin.
27. https://www.barna.org/barna-update/faith-spirituality/648-is-evangelism -going-out-of-style#.Uo9aydyVi2w.
28. George Barna, *Maximum Faith: Live Like Jesus* (Ventura, CA: Metaformation Inc.; New York: Strategenius Group LLC; Glendora, CA: WHC Publishing, 2011), 7.
29. https://www.barna.org/barna-update/culture/605-what-do-americans -really-think-about-the-bible#.Uo9r5tyVi2y.

Also by George Barna:
Revolution
Revolutionary Parenting
Master Leaders (with Bill Dallas)
The Seven Faith Tribes
Pagan Christianity? (with Frank Viola)
Futurecast
Maximum Faith
U-Turn (with David Barton)

Also by David Kinnaman:
UnChristian
You Lost Me

Assess your church's readiness
to reach out to the churchless
in your community with exclusive
Barna Group diagnostics and training.
Find out more at
www.barna.org/churchless

Barna: Cities

Knowledge to navigate a changing world

FAITH IS UNIQUE IN EVERY COMMUNITY

The spiritual vitality of the United States is deeply connected to the faith of people living in its cities. At Barna: Cities (cities.barna.org) you can find out more about the state of faith in our cities. This website offers a wealth of free information, as well as downloadable, up-to-date reports on your city or state, helping you understand and respond wisely to your region's deepest needs.

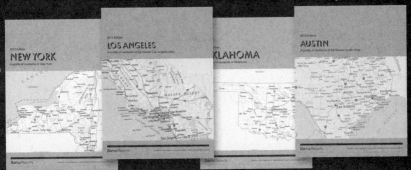

Barna Labs

TURN KNOWLEDGE INTO WISDOM WITH BARNA EVENTS

You read Barna books and subscribe to the latest research—but how do you turn data into great decisions for your church, ministry, business, or nonprofit? Join Barna Labs in person or online for new training events and learn how to transform statistics into results. Visit barna.org/labs to find out more.